GRAMMAR IN ACTION 1
An Illustrated Workbook

Barbara H. Foley
with
Gretchen M. Dowling
Union County College
Cranford, New Jersey

Heinle & Heinle Publishers
A Division of Wadsworth, Inc.
Boston, Massachusetts 02116 U.S.A.

To Bill

Director: Laurie E. Likoff
Design: A Good Thing, Inc.
Illustrations: Laura Maestro,
Felipe Galindo,
Eldon Doty
Printer and Binder: Malloy Lithographing, Inc.

GRAMMAR IN ACTION 1: An Illustrated Workbook

Library of Congress Cataloging-in-Publication Data

Foley, Barbara H.
    Grammar in action 1.

    1. English language—Textbooks for foreign
speakers.   2. English language—Grammar—
1950–   —Problems, exercises, etc.
I. Dowling, Gretchen.   II. Title.
PE1128.F56   1990   428.2'4   89-23021
ISBN 0-8384-2748-0

93   9 8 7 6

TABLE OF CONTENTS

INTRODUCTION

Grammar in Action 1 is the first in a series of three illustrated grammar workbooks for young adult and adult ESL/EFL students. It is geared for beginning level students and for those who are unfamiliar with formal grammar. Each unit is centered about a picture of a relevant everyday scene or activity. The picture captures the students' interest, introduces vocabulary, and clarifies the meaning and context of the language. Approximately eight exercises follow, four dealing with vocabulary and oral responses, and four involving writing. The final exercise in each chapter uses the target structure in connected discourse: short conversations or a reading passage. Grammar reference pages provide clear charts of the grammatical forms as well as simple explanations of meaning and usage.

WORKBOOK FEATURES

This workbook is for **beginning level students** and for those students who have had little formal grammar. In *Grammar in Action 1*, only one grammatical item is covered per unit, and it is presented in small, well-sequenced increments. Prior grammatical knowledge is not assumed, so plenty of practice on each point is provided. All contexts are pictured and the vocabulary is taught, so that the meaning is always clear and concrete. Finally, simple grammatical charts and explanations are included at the end of each unit. These are intended as reference only and can be used at any time in the unit.

Each unit centers about a **context**, that is, a picture of a relevant everday scene or activity. Initially, these pictures elicit vocabulary and motivate the students to talk about their own experiences. Within the units, the exercises are based on the picture context. The grammar exercises cannot be done mechanically, simply by filling in a word. Correctness of the grammar is tied in with the accuracy of the statement, so that the grammar is seen as meaningful.

Third, the book includes a **variety of exercises**. The exercises are carefully sequenced to guide students from a general introduction to meaningful use of the grammar. The exercises are designed to teach, not to test. They help students to visualize and figure out the grammatical pattern under discussion, as well as grasp its meaning. Additionally, the varied exercises require the students to perform different tasks. This allows for individual differences in learning styles and prevents thoughtless "mechanical" completion of exercises.

Finally, the book is a **versatile teaching tool**. It adapts to numerous teaching styles and aims. The exercises can be done in groups, individually, or as a whole class. The lessons can be used "as is," or the pictures and contexts can act as springboards for free conversation, dialog creation, dictation, or other forms of creative interaction.

THE UNITS

Each unit in the workbook follows the same format: **picture, exercises, and grammar reference charts**.

The **picture** is the core of the unit, all vocabulary, meaning, and grammar emerge from it. As the unit begins, the class should talk about the picture and what they see happening. The teacher should encourage students to volunteer information, opinions, or personal experiences related to the picture. Brief cultural explanations can be made if necessary. Some students may simply wish to give a vocabulary word or a simple sentence. In some classes, the teacher may put two or three category headings on the chalkboard, e.g., "objects," "clothes," "people," or "actions." Students then try to say any words they can from the picture. This preliminary discussion should generate student interest and clarify meanings. The focus is not correction of grammar.

In the body of the unit, there are both **speaking and writing exercises**. The speaking exercises familiarize the students with the vocabulary and grammar of the unit. Typically, the students might be asked to circle the vocabulary items they see in the picture, to read statements about the picture to decide if they are true or false, or to match a sentence and a picture. Each unit includes a chart, used to form sentences or questions about the picture. The charts help students to visualize the pattern of the structure and to include all the elements of the grammar in their sentences. Several units ask students to choose the correct form of the verb. Most speaking sections conclude with a series of questions about the picture.

The speaking exercises are instructional and clear. They give examples, show patterns, help students distinguish between two choices, and include prompt boxes. They are designed to teach the grammar and to provide the students with increasing grammatical awareness. There are many ways to utilize the speaking exercises in *Grammar in Action 1*. Depending on the students' proficiency and the teacher's personal style, the exercises may be used in a whole class, with small groups, or individually.

The writing exercises provide an opportunity for the students to work alone or in pairs. These exercises are contextualized. Students are directed to fill in sentences with the correct word, to place words in the correct order to form a sentence, or to answer questions about the context. Beginning with Unit 11, the final exercise is a story related to the context. After they read the story, the students answer questions or form the questions themselves.

The writing exercises may be used as an in-class assignment or as homework. In the first few units, it will be necessary to do several examples of each exercise together as a class. Once students are familiar with the written assignments, they will not need this support. All written exercises should be corrected in class. During this time, the teacher can answer questions and further assess the students' understanding of the grammar.

At the conclusion of each unit are one or more **grammar boxes**, outlining the grammar which is included in the unit. The grammar boxes are not "taught" or memorized but are provided as a reference. When using them, it is helpful to have the students "read" sentences from the boxes. Students can then be encouraged to give other examples from the unit they are studying or from their own lives.

IN CONCLUSION

Grammar in Action 1 is a grammar workbook. The picture contexts are the starting points. The exercises then provide clear and thorough grammar practice. Additionally, teachers will want to use these units as springboards for directed discussions, free conversations, dialog activities, and other creative interactions. The teachers can use the students' language to expand the units and to meet the interests and needs of their particular English language classes.

ACKNOWLEDGMENTS

We wish to thank the ESL staff and students of Union County College, New Jersey, for their support and encouragement during this project. We would especially like to thank Howard Pomann for his suggestions, and Marinna Kolaitis, Dorothy Burak, and Deborah Pires for the hours they spent listening and caring.

AT SCHOOL

Be Statements of Location

1. _____

2. _____

3. _____

4. _____

5. _____

A. Write these words under the correct picture.

at school	in class
at home	in Room 2
at work	

I   you   you   he   she   we   they

B. Draw a line from the person(s) to the correct place.

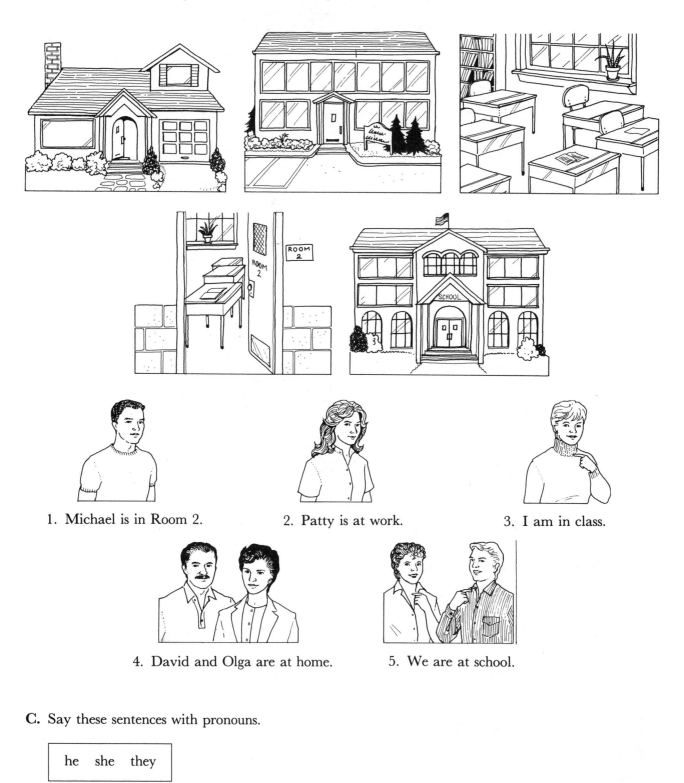

1. Michael is in Room 2.

2. Patty is at work.

3. I am in class.

4. David and Olga are at home.

5. We are at school.

C. Say these sentences with pronouns.

| he she they |

Example: Patty is at work.
She is at work.

1. Michael is in Room 2.
2. David and Olga are at home.
3. Patty is at work.
4. Ali is in Room 2.
5. Don is at work.

6. The students are in class.
7. Teresa is in class.
8. Ann is in Room 2.
9. Kim and Susan are at school.
10. Paul is at home.

D. Say these sentences with contractions.

Examples: She is in class.   He is not at home.
            She's in class.   He isn't at home.

1. He is at home.
2. I am at school.
3. She is at work.
4. They are in class.
5. We are in Room 2.

6. He is not at work.
7. You are not in Room 2.
8. I am not at home.
9. We are not in class.
10. They are not in Room 2.

E. Look at the pictures in Exercise B. Correct these statements.

Example: Patty is at home.
             Patty isn't at home.
             She's at work.

1. Michael is at home.
2. Patty is at school.
3. David and Olga are in class.
4. We are at work.
5. I'm at home.

6. Michael is at work.
7. We're at home.
8. David and Olga are in Room 2.
9. Patty is in class.
10. I'm at work.

Writing

A. Fill in each blank with the correct word.

am	is	are

1. He __is__ in Room 2.

2. They _____ at home.

3. I _____ in class.

4. You _____ in Room 2.

5. She _____ at work.

6. We _____ in school.

7. I _____ at home.

8. We _____ at work.

9. She _____ in class.

10. I _____ at home.

11. You _____ at school.

12. He _____ in Room 2.

13. They _____ at work.

14. I _____ at school.

B. Write these sentences with contractions.

1. I am in class.   *I'm in class.*

2. They are at home.   _____

3. She is at work.   _____

4. We are at school.   _____

5. He is in Room 2.   _____

6. You are at school.   _____

7. I am at work.   _____

8. She is in class.   _____

9. They are at home.   _____

10. You are in class.   _____

C. Write these sentences with pronouns.

1. Michael is in Room 2.   *He's in Room 2.*

2. Patty is at work.   _____

3. David and Olga are at home. _____

4. Ann and Patty are at work. _____

5. Paul is in Room 2.   _____

6. Kim is at work.   _____

7. Patty and Kim are at work. _____

8. Ali is at home.   _____

9. Teresa is at home.   _____

10. Paul is at school.   _____

D. Correct these sentences.

Example:

Patty is at work.

Patty isn't at work.
She's in school.

1.

Ali is at work.

_____

_____

2.

I'm at school.

_____

_____

3.

Ann and Patty are at work.

_____

_____

4.

You're in class.

_____

_____

5.

Teresa is in Room 2.

_____

_____

6.

We're at home.

_____

_____

7. _____

Paul is in class. _____

8. _____

Kim is in Room 5. _____

9. _____

David and Olga are at home. _____

10. _____

I'm at work. _____

Grammar Summary

I	am		
We You They	are	not	in class. at home.
He She It	is		

Contractions

I am	⟶	I'm
He is	⟶	He's
She is	⟶	She's
It is	⟶	It's
You are	⟶	You're
They are	⟶	They're
We are	⟶	We're
is not	⟶	isn't
are not	⟶	aren't

OCCUPATIONS

Be Statements of Identification

A. Write the name of each person under his or her picture.

1. Paul and Olga are factory workers.
2. Michael is an engineer.
3. Kim and Ann are students.
4. Ann is an accountant.
5. Patty is a nurse.

6. Teresa and Lee are cashiers.
7. Harry is a teacher.
8. David is a police officer.
9. Mary is a dentist.
10. Kim is a housewife.

B. Read each sentence and circle "Yes" or "No."

1. Ann is a factory worker.   Yes   (No)
2. Mary is a dentist.   Yes   No
3. Harry is a nurse.   Yes   No
4. Teresa and Lee are police officers.   Yes   No
5. Michael is an engineer.   Yes   No
6. Kim is an accountant.   Yes   No
7. Kim and Ann are students.   Yes   No
8. David is a cashier.   Yes   No
9. Patty is a teacher.   Yes   No
10. Paul and Olga are nurses.   Yes   No

C. Circle the correct word(s) under each picture.

1.

a nurse
(nurses)

2.

a teacher
teachers

3.

a factory worker
factory workers

4.

a cashier
cashiers

5.

an engineer
engineers

6.

a student
students

7.

a housewife
housewives

8.

a police officer
police officers

8

D. Tell each person's occupation.

Example: She's a teacher.

Writing

A. Circle the correct answer.

1. I'm (a student)/students.
2. He's **an engineer**/engineers.
3. Donna and Jim are **a nurse**/nurses.
4. Mary and Alice are **a housewife**/housewives.
5. She's **a teacher**/teachers.
6. We are **a student**/students.
7. David is **a police officer**/police officers.
8. Don is **a cashier**/cashiers.
9. They're **a factory worker**/factory workers.
10. Sam and Wanda are **an accountant**/accountants.

B. Fill in each blank with the correct word or letter.

am	a
is	an
are	s

1. I _____ *am a* _____ student.

2. Kathy and Bill _____ police officer _____.

3. They _____ nurse _____.

4. Kim _____ _____ housewife.

5. Bill and Barbara _____ teacher _____.

6. Tony and Lee _____ cashier _____.

7. He _____ _____ factory worker.

8. John _____ _____ dentist.

9. We _____ student _____.

10. Michael _____ _____ engineer.

C. Put the words in these sentences in the correct order.

1. a / is / . / Tom / teacher

   Tom is a teacher. _____

2. student / I / am / . / a

   _____

3. is / She / . / housewife / a

   _____

4. Kim / students / are / . / and / Teresa

   _____

5. police officer / a / Ken / . / is

   _____

6. . / Patty / a / is / nurse

   _____

7. students / . / are / We

   _____

10

8. and / Susan / . / Ellen / teachers / are

_____

9. an / is / . / He / accountant

_____

10. engineers / . / They / are

_____

D. Write a sentence about each picture.

1. <u>*They are cashiers.*</u>   2. _____

3. _____   4. _____

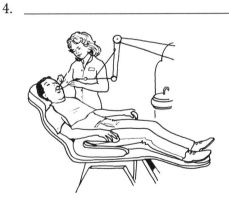

5. _____   6. _____

7. _____

8. _____

9. _____

10. _____

Grammar Summary

I	am	a	nurse.
	am not		
He She It	is isn't	an	a _____. e _____. i _____. o _____. u _____.
You	are aren't		
We You They	are aren't		_____s.

I	am		a	_____.
He She It	is	not	an	a _____. e _____. i _____. o _____.
You	are			u _____.
We You They	are			_____s.

Notes

Singular: one (1)
Nouns with **a** or **an** are singular.

Plural: two (2) or more (+)
Nouns with **s** are plural.

FEELINGS

Be Statements of Description
Yes / No Questions with Be

A. Write the name of each student under his/her picture.

1. Michael is tired.
2. David and Ali are thirsty.
3. Patty is sick.
4. Olga is nervous.
5. Paul and Teresa are cold.
6. Kim is hot.
7. Ann is hungry.

B. Look at the picture in Exercise A. Circle the correct answer.

1. Is Michael tired?	(Yes, he is.)	No, he isn't.
2. Is Michael thirsty?	Yes, he is.	No, he isn't.
3. Are David and Ali hungry?	Yes, they are.	No, they aren't.
4. Are David and Ali sick?	Yes, they are.	No, they aren't.
5. Is Patty thirsty?	Yes, she is.	No, she isn't.
6. Is Patty sick?	Yes, she is.	No, she isn't.
7. Is Olga nervous?	Yes, she is.	No, she isn't.
8. Are Paul and Teresa cold?	Yes, they are.	No, they aren't.
9. Is Kim cold?	Yes, she is.	No, she isn't.
10. Is Ann hungry?	Yes, she is.	No, she isn't.

C. Answer these questions about yourself.

> Yes, I am.   No, I'm not.

1. Are you tired?
2. Are you thirsty?
3. Are you sick?
4. Are you nervous?
5. Are you cold?
6. Are you hot?
7. Are you hungry?

D. Ask and answer questions about the students in the picture.

Example: Is Michael **tired?** Yes, he is.
Is Michael **cold?** No, he isn't.

1. Is Patty_____?
2. Is Patty_____?
3. Are David and Ali_____?
4. Are David and Ali_____?
5. Is Olga_____?
6. Is Olga_____?
7. Are Paul and Teresa_____?
8. Are Paul and Teresa_____?
9. Is Kim_____?
10. Is Ann_____?

14

Writing

A. Answer the questions about each picture.

1. Is Michael tired?   *Yes, he is.*

2. Is Michael hungry?   _____, _____ _____.

3. Is Kim nervous?   _____, _____ _____.

4. Is Kim hot?   _____, _____ _____.

5. Are David and Ali hungry?   _____, _____ _____.

6. Are David and Ali thirsty?   _____, _____ _____.

7. Is Patty sick?   _____, _____ _____.

8. Is Patty cold?   _____, _____ _____.

9. Are Paul and Teresa cold? _____ , _____ _____ .

10. Are Paul and Teresa hot? _____ , _____ _____ .

B. Put the words in the correct order. Then, answer the question.

1. Patty / ? / Is / sick

    Is Patty sick ?   *Yes, she is.*

2. nervous / Is / ? / Olga

    _____   _____

3. ? / Paul / Teresa / sick / Are / and

    _____   _____

4. thirsty / Kim / Is / ?

    _____   _____

5. ? / David / and / nervous / Ali / Are

    _____   _____

6. Ann / ? / Is / hungry

    _____   _____

7. tired / Michael / ? / Is

    _____   _____

8. Olga / ? / tired / Is

    _____   _____

9. cold / and / Paul / ? / Are / Teresa

    _____   _____

10. Is / thirsty / Patty / ?

    _____   _____

C. Fill in these conversations.

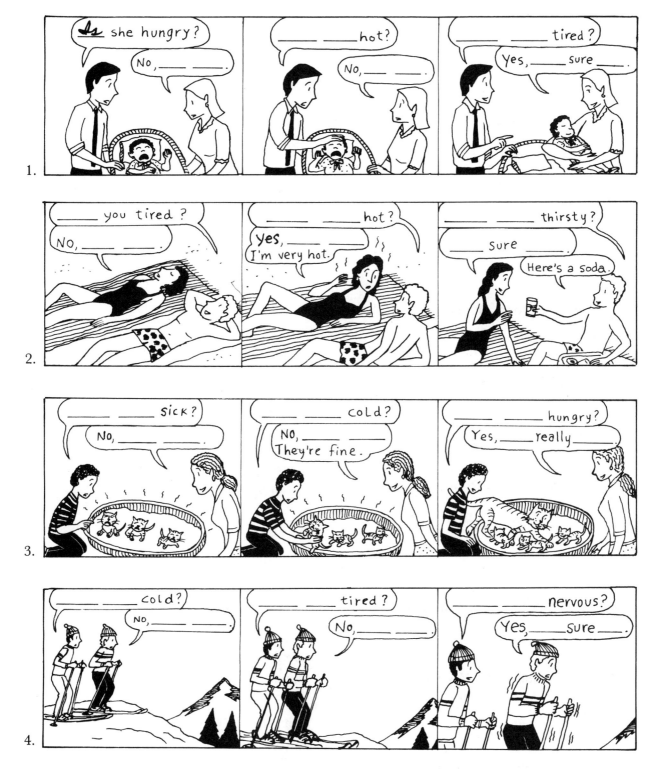

Grammar Summary

Be Statements of Description:

I	am am not	**sick.**
We You They	are are not	**tired.**
He She It	is is not	**late.**

Yes / No Questions with Be

Are you tired? . . . . Yes, I am.
Is Patty sick? . . . . Yes, she is.
Is Paul sick? . . . . No, he isn't.
Are Paul and Teresa nervous? . . . . No, they aren't.

Am	I	**sick?**
Are	we you they	**tired?**
Is	he she it	**late?**

Questions: Short Answers with Be

Am I		Yes, you are.	No, you aren't.
Are we	**sick?**	Yes, you are.	No, you aren't.
Are you	**late?**	Yes, I am. Yes, we are.	No, I'm not. No, we aren't.
Are they		Yes, they are.	No, they aren't.
Is he	**old?**	Yes, he is.	No, he isn't.
Is she		Yes, she is.	No, she isn't.
Is it		Yes, it is.	No, it isn't.

REGISTRATION

Or and Wh Questions with Be

A. Look at the new students and answer these questions.

Examples: Who is tall?   George is. **or**
                                George and Robert are.

1. Who is thin?
2. Who is married?
3. Who is young?
4. Who is middle-aged?

5. Who is single?
6. Who is heavy?
7. Who is tall?
8. Who is short?

B. Circle the correct answer.

1. Is George tall?   (Yes, he is.)   No, he isn't.
2. Is George old or young?   He's young.   No, he isn't.
3. Is George heavy?   Yes, he is.   No, he isn't.
4. Is Ellen married?   Yes, she is.   No, she isn't.
5. Is Ellen thin?   Yes, she is.   No, she isn't.
6. Is Ellen tall or short?   She's tall.   Yes, she is.
7. Is Linda old, young, or middle-aged?   She's middle-aged.   No, she isn't.
8. Are Linda and Robert old?   Yes, they are.   No, they aren't.
9. Is Robert short?   He's short.   No, he isn't.
10. Is Robert thin or heavy?   He's thin.   No, he isn't.

C. Answer these questions about the new students.

Example: Is George young? **Yes, he is.**

1. Is George tall?
2. Is George thin or heavy?
3. Is Ellen married?
4. Is Ellen tall or short?
5. Are Ellen and George tall?
6. Is Linda short?
7. Is Linda old, young, or middle-aged?
8. Is Robert old?
9. Is Robert tall or short?
10. Is Robert thin or heavy?

D. Answer the questions about the registration forms.

Example: Where is George from?
     He's from Mexico.

Name	George Garcia
Country	Mexico
Class	ESL 1
Teacher	Mr. Gibson

1. Where is George from?
2. What class is he in?
3. Who is his teacher?

Name	Ellen Mikos
Country	Greece
Class	ESL 3
Teacher	Mrs. Bond

4. Where is Ellen from?
5. What class is she in?
6. Who is her teacher?

Name LINDA CHO	
Country CHINA	
Class TYPING 1	7. Where is Linda from?
Teacher MISS ROBERTS	8. What class is she in?
	9. Who is her teacher?

Name Robert Remy	
Country Haiti	
Class Auto Mechanics	10. Where is Robert from?
Teacher Mr. Reed	11. What class is he in?
	12. Who is his teacher?

Writing

A. Look at the picture on page 19 and answer the questions.

1. Is George tall or short? _He's tall._

2. Is George tall? _____

3. Is George short? _____

4. Is Ellen young? _____

5. Is Ellen thin? _____

6. Is Linda heavy or thin? _____

7. Is Linda heavy? _____

8. Is Linda thin? _____

9. Is Robert heavy or thin? _____

10. Is Robert tall or short? _____

B. Put the words in the correct order. Then, answer the question.

1. George / young / Is / ? / old / or

   Is George old or young?   *He's young.*

2. Is / heavy / ? / George

   _____   _____

3. ? / old / George / Is

   _____   _____

4. heavy / Is / ? / Ellen

   _____   _____

5. tall / short / ? / Ellen / or / Is

   _____   _____

6. Linda / thin / or / Is / ? / heavy?

   _____   _____

7. Is / tall / Linda / ?

   _____   _____

8. Robert / thin / Is / heavy / or / ?

   _____   _____

9. young / ? / Is / Robert

   _____   _____

10. Robert / George / tall / ? / Are / and

    _____   _____

C. Fill in each blank with the correct word.

What	Where	Who

1. *Where* _____ is George from?   Mexico.

2. _____ is his teacher?   Mr. Gibson.

3. _____ class is he in?   ESL 1.

4. _____ is Ellen from?   Greece.

5. _____ class is she in?   ESL 3.

6. _____ is her teacher?   Mrs. Bond

7. _____ is Linda from?   China.

8. _____ is her teacher?   Miss Roberts.

9. _____ is Robert from?   Haiti.

10. _____ is his teacher?   Mr. Reed.

D. Read this story. Then, answer the questions.

Robert Remy is a new student in this school. He's from Haiti. Robert is 25 years old. He's tall and thin. Robert is very friendly. He isn't married.

Robert is in two night classes. He is in ESL 1 at 7:00. His teacher is Mr. Gibson. Robert is in Auto Mechanics at 8:30. His teacher is Mr. Reed.

1. Where is Robert from?   _Haiti._____

2. Is he a new student?   _____

3. Is he old or young?   _____

4. Is he 35 years old?   _____

5. Is Robert tall or short?   _____

6. Is he friendly?   _____

7. Is Robert in four classes?   _____

8. What class is he in at 7:00?   _____

9. What class is he in at 8:30?   _____

10. Who is his teacher in Auto Mechanics?   _____

Grammar Summary

OR Questions

Is Ellen married or single?   She's married.
Is Robert married or single?   He's single.
Is Ellen married?   Yes, she is.
Is Robert married?   No, he isn't.

Am	I	
Is	he/she/it	_____or_____ ?
Are	we/you/they	

WH Questions

Where is Robert from? . . . . Haiti.
What class is he in? . . . . ESL 1.
Who is his teacher? . . . . Mr. Gibson.

Where	is	he/she/it	from?
	are	you/they	

I	am		city.
He/She/It	is	from	state.
We/You/They	are		country.

What	room class ___	am	I	in?
		is	he/she/it	
		are	we/you/they	

I	am		Room 2.
He/She/It	is	in	ESL 1.
We/You/They	are		

Who	is	tall?
George	is.	
George and Ellen	are.	

UNIT 5
IN THE HALL

This / That / These / Those

A. Circle the items you see on the floor.

(book)	flowers	wallet
cup	dictionary	gloves
coat	radio	paper
notebook	hat	umbrella
pens	pencils	keys

B. Circle the sentence for each picture.

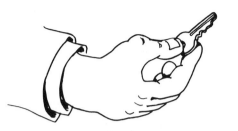

1. Is this your key?
   Is that your key?

2. Is this your key?
   Is that your key?

3. Are these your keys?
   Are those your keys?

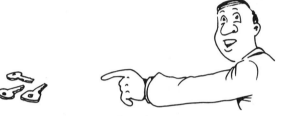

4. Are these your keys?
   Are those your keys?

5. Is this your dictionary?
   Is that your dictionary?

6. Is this your dictionary?
   Is that your dictionary?

7. Are these your gloves?
   Are those your gloves?

8. Are these your gloves?
   Are those your gloves?

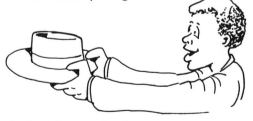

9. Is this your hat?
   Is that your hat?

10. Is this your hat?
    Is that your hat?

C. Ask and answer questions about these items.

Is this/that your _____?
Yes, it is.   No, it isn't.

1.

2.

3.

4.

5.

6.

D. Ask and answer questions about these items.

Are these / those your_____?
Yes, they are.   No, they aren't.

1.

2.

3.

4.

5.

6.

Writing

A. Draw a stick figure to show each question.

This

That

1. Is this your hat?

2. Are those your keys?

3. Is this your wallet?

4. Is that your book?

5. Are these your papers?

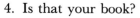

6. Is this your pen?

7. Are those your gloves?

8. Is that your umbrella?

9. Is that your briefcase?

10. Are these your pencils?

B. Circle the correct answer.

1. Is this your dictionary?   (Yes, it is.)   Yes, they are.
2. Are these your books?   Yes, it is.   Yes, they are.
3. Is that your wallet?   No, it isn't.   No, they aren't.
4. Is this your hat?   Yes, it is.   Yes, they are.
5. Are those your pencils?   No, it isn't.   No, they aren't.
6. Are these your keys?   Yes, it is.   Yes, they are.
7. Is this your briefcase?   Yes, it is.   Yes, they are.
8. Are those your papers?   No, it isn't.   No, they aren't.
9. Is that your book?   Yes, it is.   Yes, they are.
10. Is this your pen?   No, it isn't.   No, they aren't.

C. Complete these conversations.

Grammar Summary

The Demonstrative Pronouns: This, That, These, Those

This

That

These

Those

Is this your* book? . . . . .Yes, it is.
Is that your book? . . . . .No, it isn't.
Are these your books? . . . . .Yes, they are.
Are those your books? . . . . .No, they aren't.

Is	this	your _____?
	that	

Singular: 1 thing

Yes,	it	is.
No,		isn't.
		's not.

Are	these	your_____s?
	those	

Plural: 2 or more things

Yes,	they	are.
No,		aren't.
		're not.

*See page 36 for possessives.

30

Possessive Nouns and Adjectives

Joe   Rose

David's Family

Stella   David   Olga

Jeff   Kathy

A. This is David's family. Write the correct word under each person.

son	daughter	sister
mother	father	wife

B. Read each sentence and circle **Yes** or **No**.

1. Stella is David's sister.	(Yes)	No	7. David is Joe's brother.	Yes	No
2. Stella is Kathy's aunt.	Yes	No	8. David is Rose's son.	Yes	No
3. Stella is Joe's daughter.	Yes	No	9. Rose is Joe's wife.	Yes	No
4. Stella is Jeff's mother.	Yes	No	10. Rose is Olga's mother.	Yes	No
5. David is Olga's husband.	Yes	No	11. Rose is Stella's aunt.	Yes	No
6. David is Kathy's father.	Yes	No	12. Rose is Jeff's grandmother.	Yes	No

C. Answer these questions about David's family.

Example: Who is David's father? Joe is.

1. Who is David's son?
2. Who is David's wife?
3. Who is Olga's husband?
4. Who is Olga's daughter?
5. Who is Stella's mother?

6. Who is Stella's brother?
7. Who is Kathy's grandmother?
8. Who is Kathy's aunt?
9. Who is Joe's son?
10. Who is Joe's grandson?

D. Give the name of each person.

his	her	their

Example:

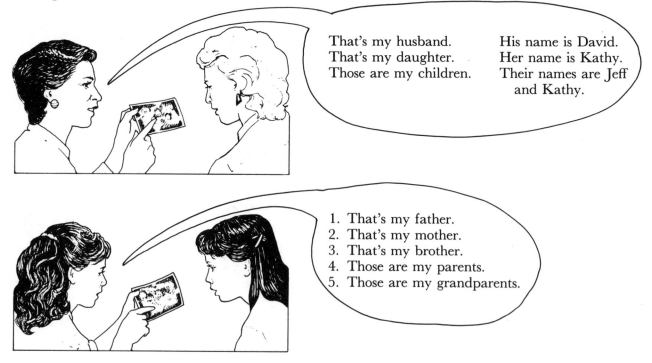

That's my husband.   His name is David.
That's my daughter.   Her name is Kathy.
Those are my children.   Their names are Jeff and Kathy.

1. That's my father.
2. That's my mother.
3. That's my brother.
4. Those are my parents.
5. Those are my grandparents.

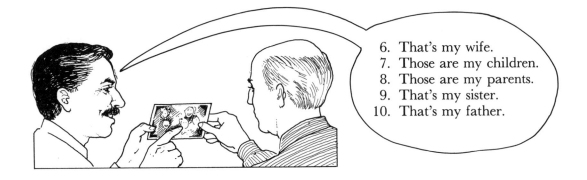

6. That's my wife.
7. Those are my children.
8. Those are my parents.
9. That's my sister.
10. That's my father.

Writing

A. This is Olga's family. Answer the questions about her family.

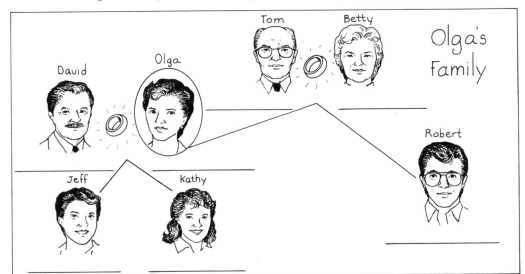

1. Who is Olga's husband?   *David is.*

2. Who is Olga's father?   _____

3. Who is Olga's mother?   _____

4. Who is Olga's brother?   _____

5. Who is Olga's son?   _____

6. Who is Jeff's father?   _____

7. Who is Jeff's grandfather?   _____

8. Who is Jeff's grandmother?_____

9. Who is Jeff's uncle?   _____

10. Who is Jeff's sister?   _____

33

B. Fill in the blanks about Olga's family.

1. Olga is ___*David's*___ wife.

2. Olga is _____ sister.

3. David is _____ father.

4. David is _____ husband.

5. Robert is _____ son.

6. Robert is _____ uncle.

7. Kathy is _____ daughter.

8. Kathy is _____ sister.

9. Betty is _____ grandmother.

10. Betty is _____ wife.

C. Give the name of each person in Olga's family.

his	her	their

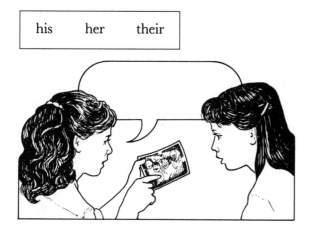

1. That's my mother.

   *Her name is Olga.*

2. That's my uncle.

   _____

3. That's my brother.

   _____

4. Those are my parents.

   _____

5. Those are my grandparents.

   _____

6. That's my husband.

   _____

7. Those are my children.

   _____

8. That's my brother.

   _____

9. Those are my parents.

   _____

10. That's my daughter.

   _____

34

D. Draw a simple picture of your family. Write the name of each person under his/her picture. Write ten sentences about the relationships in your family.

1. _____
2. _____
3. _____
4. _____
5. _____
6. _____
7. _____
8. _____
9. _____
10. _____

Grammar Summary

Possessives

Nouns: **'s** = singular possessive
Adjectives: **my, your, his, her, our, their**

Question: Short Answer:
Who is Olga's husband? . . . . David is.

Who	is	Name's my/your/his her/our/their	_____?	Name is. Name + Name are.

Statements:

David is Olga's husband.   Olga is David's wife.
Jeff is her son.   Jeff is his son.
Kathy is her daughter.   Kathy is his daughter.
They are her children.   They are his children.
        Kathy is their daughter.
        Jeff is their son.

Name He She That	is	Name's my/your/his her/our/their	teacher. friend.
Name + Name They Those	are		teachers. friends. children.

That is my husband.   His name is David.
Those are my children.   Their names are Kathy and Jeff.
That is my daughter.   Her name is Kathy.

My Your His	name teacher	is	Name.
Her Our Their	names teachers _____	are	Name and Name.

Plural possessives:
's is possessive for irregular plurals.
    Example: the children's mother
' is possessive for plurals with "s".
    Example: the boys' father

THE CLOTHING STORE

How much is it? How much are they?*

A. Read these sentences. Write the prices in the ad.

Example: The shorts are $10.
The shorts are ten dollars.

1. The shirt is $8.
2. The sneakers are $17.
3. The socks are $3.
4. The dress is $46.
5. The jacket is $49.

6. The hat is $12.
7. The heels are $64.
8. The panty hose are $4.
9. The necklace is $19.
10. The earrings are $12.

11. The shirt is $25.
12. The tie is $7.
13. The belt is $9.
14. The pants are $29.
15. The shoes are $39.

*See appendix, page 137, for numbers.

B. Circle the clothes that your classmates are wearing.

jeans	blouse	shorts	sweater
skirt	sneakers	socks	earrings
pants	dress	tie	shoes
jacket	shirt	sandals	hat
boots	belt	necklace	

C. Circle the correct answer.

1. How much is this hat? — (It's $25.) — They're $25.
2. How much are these shoes? — It's $44. — (They're $44.)
3. How much are these sneakers? — It's $17. — They're $17.
4. How much is this jacket? — It's $49. — They're $49.
5. How much is this dress? — It's $56. — They're $56.
6. How much are these shorts? — It's $11. — They're $11.
7. How much is this shirt? — It's $18. — They're $18.
8. How much are these pants? — It's $29. — They're $29.
9. How much are these socks? — It's $ 3. — They're $ 3.
10. How much is this belt? — It's $12. — They're $12.

D. Ask and answer questions about the price of each item below.
Make up your own prices.

Examples: How much is this hat? — It's $12. (It's twelve dollars.)
How much are these earrings? — They're $20. (They're twenty dollars.)

1.

2.

3.

4.

5.

6.

7.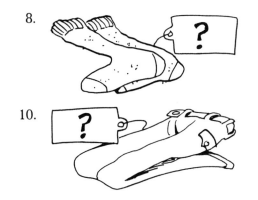

8.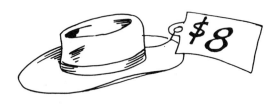

9.

10.

Writing

A. Write a sentence about each item.

1. *These shoes are $44.*

2. *This hat is $8.*

$18

3. _____

$46

4. _____

$25

5. _____

$11

6. _____

$9

7. _____

$50

8. _____

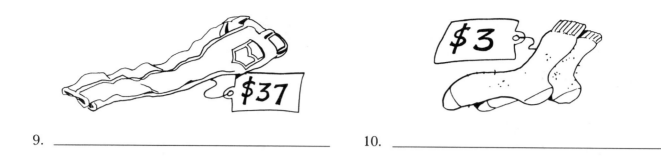

9. _____   10. _____

B. Write a price on each item. Then, answer the question.

1. How much is this hat?

_It's_ _____

2. How much are these shoes?

They're _____

3. How much are these earrings?

_____

4. How much is this shirt?

_____

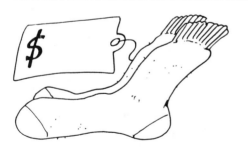

5. How much are these socks?

_____

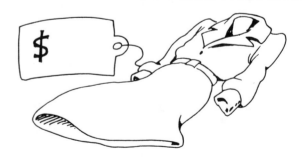

6. How much is this dress?

_____

7. How much is this jacket?

_____

8. How much are these jeans?

_____

9. How much are these shorts?

_____

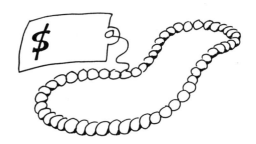

10. How much is this necklace?

_____

C. Fill in the conversations.

1.

How much _is_ _this_ _shirt_?

IT'S on sale. ___ $15.

2.

How much ___ ___ ___?

They're on sale. ___ $___.

3.

This is a beautiful necklace.

Yes, ___. ___ $75

That's expensive.

4.

___ on sale?

No, it's ___. ___ $100.

___ JACKETS ___ on sale. ___ $50.

Grammar Summary

Prices:

How much is this hat . . . . It's $10.00 (ten dollars).
How much are these shoes? . . . . They're $40.00 (forty dollars).

How much	is	this	_____?
	are	these	_____s?

Singular	This _____ It	is	$xx.00. (_____ dollars.)
Plural	These _____ They _____	are	

42

Prepositions
Where questions review

A. Write the furniture under the correct room.

✓sofa	end table	armchair	table
✓stove	refrigerator	cabinets	toilet
dresser	coffee table	counter	bed
chairs	night table	bathtub	
sink	television		

Bedroom   **Bathroom**   **Living Room**   **Kitchen**

sofa   *stove*

| in | on | next to | between | under | over |

B. Draw these things in the house on page 43.

Bedroom

1. Put a clock radio on the dresser.

2. Put a small photo next to the clock radio.

3. Put two shoes under the bed.

Bathroom

4. Put a mirror over the sink.

Living Room

5. Put a tall lamp next to the sofa.

6. Put some flowers on the television.

Kitchen

7. Put a toaster on the counter next to the refrigerator.

8. Put a clock over the refrigerator.

9. Put a bowl on the table.

10. Put three apples in the bowl.

C. Read each sentence about the house and circle "Yes" or "No."

1. The lights are over the bed.   (Yes)   No
2. The pictures are on the wall in the bedroom.   Yes   No
3. The photo is next to the clock radio.   Yes   No
4. The mirror is over the toilet.   Yes   No
5. The toilet is between the sink and the bathtub.   Yes   No
6. The lamp is next to the sofa.   Yes   No
7. The shoes are on the bed.   Yes   No
8. The flowers are on the television.   Yes   No
9. The toaster is under the refrigerator.   Yes   No
10. The telephone is on the wall in the kitchen.   Yes   No

D. Answer these questions about the house.

Examples: Where's the photo?   It's next to the clock radio.
           Where are the apples?   They're in the bowl.

1. Where's the dresser?
2. Where's the night table?
3. Where's the small photo?
4. Where are the lights?
5. Where are the shoes?

6. Where's the television?
7. Where are the flowers?
8. Where's the end table?
9. Where are the pictures?
10. Where's the toaster?

Writing

A. Fill in each blank with the correct preposition.

in	on	next to	under	over	between

1. The dresser is _____*in*_____ the bedroom.

2. The shoes are _____ the bed.

3. The clock radio is _____ the photo.

4. The night table is _____ the bed and the dresser.

5. The sink is _____ the toilet.

6. The mirror is _____ the sink.

7. The end table is _____ the sofa.

8. The sofa is _____ the living room.

9. The pictures are _____ the sofa.

10. The flowers are _____ the television.

11. The telephone is _____ the wall.

12. The bowl is _____ the table.

13. The clock is _____ the refrigerator.

14. The cabinets are _____ the kitchen.

15. The toaster is _____ the refrigerator.

B. Ask and answer questions about this kitchen.

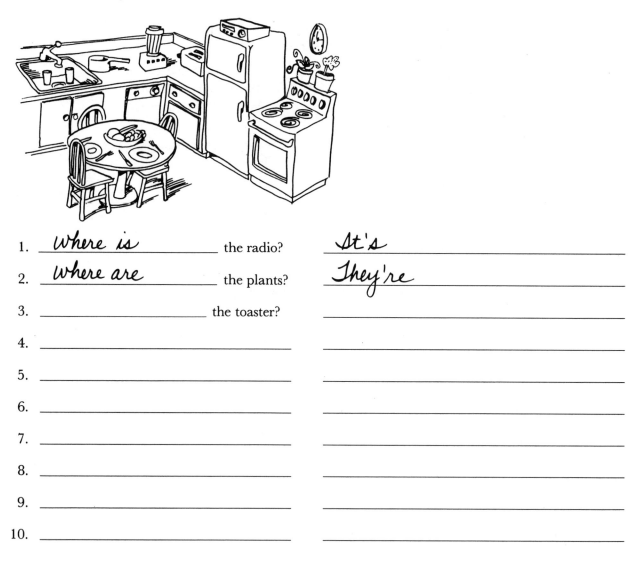

1. __*Where is*_____ the radio?   *It's* _____

2. __*Where are*_____ the plants?   *They're* _____

3. _____ the toaster?   _____

4. _____   _____

5. _____   _____

6. _____   _____

7. _____   _____

8. _____   _____

9. _____   _____

10. _____   _____

C. Bob's room is always a mess. Where are his things?

> MOM, WHERE'S MY SOCCER BALL?
>
> I THINK IT'S IN YOUR CLOSET.

1. Where's my soccer ball?   *I think it's in your closet.*

2. Where's my radio? _____

3. Where's my belt? _____

4. Where's my tennis racket? _____

5. Where's my wallet? _____

6. Where's my calendar? _____

7. Where are my sneakers? _____

8. Where's my backpack? _____

9. Where's my tie? _____

10. Where's my telephone? _____

D. Answer these questions about your house.

1. Where's your telephone?   *It's* _____

2. Where's your television? _____

3. Where's your clock radio? _____

4. Where's your calendar? _____

5. Where's your stereo? _____

47

Grammar Summary

Prepositions of Place:

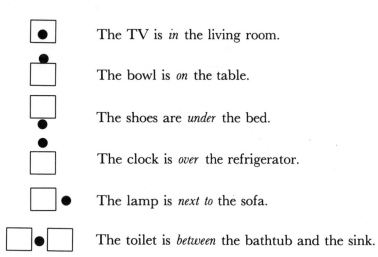

The TV is *in* the living room.

The bowl is *on* the table.

The shoes are *under* the bed.

The clock is *over* the refrigerator.

The lamp is *next to* the sofa.

The toilet is *between* the bathtub and the sink.

Where	is	the _____?
	are	the _____s?

The _____	is	in on over	the _____.
It			
The _____s	are	under	
They		between the _____ and the _____.	

More Prepositions

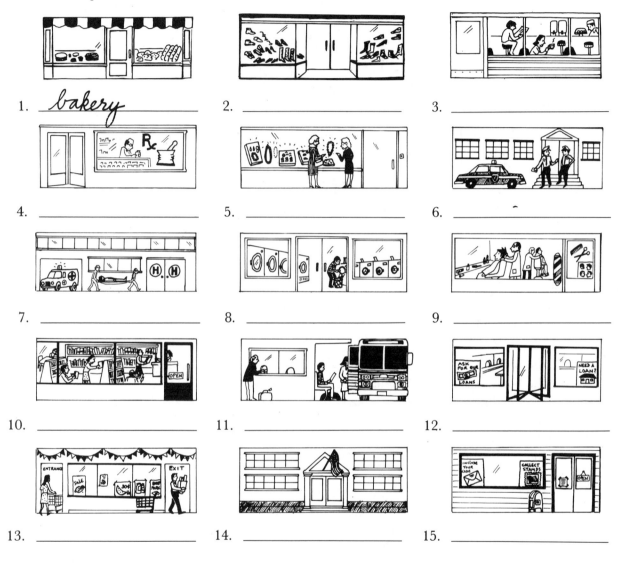

1. *bakery*

2. _____

3. _____

4. _____

5. _____

6. _____

7. _____

8. _____

9. _____

10. _____

11. _____

12. _____

13. _____

14. _____

15. _____

A. Write the name of the place under the correct picture.

shoe store	hospital	drugstore
bus station	bank	diner
supermarket	library	jewelry store
police station	laundromat	post office
high school	barber shop	✓ bakery

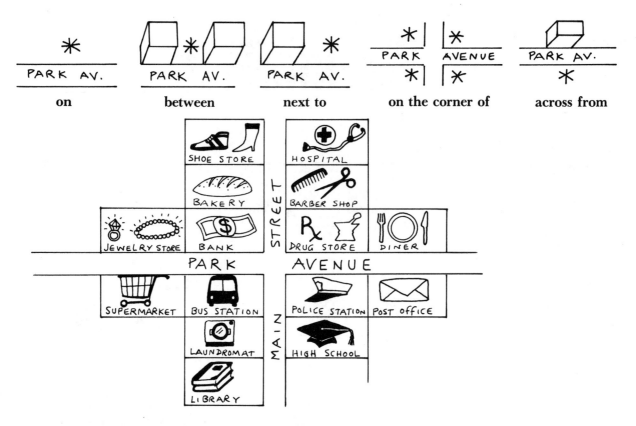

on	between	next to	on the corner of	across from

B. Look at the map above and answer the questions.

> **Example:** What's the building on Main Street, between the drug-store and the hospital?
> **The barber shop.**

1. What's the building on Main Street, between the drugstore and the hospital?
2. What's the building on Park Avenue, across from the post office?
3. What's the building on Park Avenue, next to the bus station?
4. What's the building on the corner of Main Street and Park Avenue? (Four answers are correct.)
5. What's the building on Main Street, across from the hospital?
6. What's the building on Main Street, between the library and the bus station?
7. What's the building on Main Street, next to the hospital?
8. What's the building on Park Avenue, next to the diner?
.9. What's the building on Main Street, between the bank and the shoe store?
10. What's the building on Main Street, across from the high school?

C. Give the location of each building.

> **Example:** Where's the post office?
> **It's on Park Avenue, next to the police station.**

1. Where's the drugstore?
2. Where's the bank?
3. Where's the supermarket?
4. Where's the laundromat?
5. Where's the diner?
6. Where's the library?
7. Where's the barber shop?
8. Where's the bus station?
9. Where's the police station?
10. Where's the shoe store?

Writing

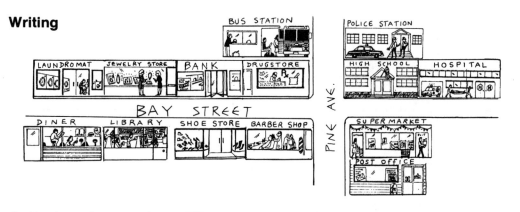

A. Look at the map above. Fill in each blank with the correct word(s).

on	on the corner of
between	across from
next to	

1. The bank is _____*between*_____ the jewelry store and the drugstore.

2. The bus station is _____ the police station.

3. The high school is _____ Pine Avenue and Bay Street.

4. The library is _____ Bay Street.

5. The barber shop is _____ Pine Avenue and Bay Street.

6. The jewelry store is _____ the laundromat.

7. The post office is _____ Pine Avenue.

8. The hospital is _____ the high school.

9. The shoe store is _____ the bank.

10. The shoe store is _____ the barber shop and the library.

B. Write about five buildings on the map above.

1. _____*The bank is next to the drugstore.*_____

2. _____

3. _____

4. _____

5. _____

C. Read the location of each store. Write the store names on the map.

		Post Office	Bank		

B R O A D   S T R E E T

		Super-market			

1. The post office is on Broad Street, across from the supermarket.
2. The bank is between the post office and the bus station.
3. The laundromat is across from the bus station.
4. The police station is across from the bank.
5. The supermarket is between the barber shop and the police station.
6. The high school is on Broad Street, next to the laundromat.
7. The jewelry store is across from the barber shop.
8. The shoe store is next to the jewelry store and across from the library.
9. The library is on Broad Street, across from the shoe store.
10. The bus station is between the bank and the diner.

D. Write the location of these buildings in your town.

1. My school is _____ .

2. The post office is _____ .

3. The hospital is _____ .

4. The high school is _____ .

5. The police station is _____ .

Grammar Summary

More Prepositions of Place:

The jewelry store is *on* Park Avenue.   The bakery is *between* the bank and the drugstore.

The jewelry store is *next to* the bank.   The bank is *on the corner* of Main Street and Park Avenue.

The supermarket is *across from* the jewelry store.

The _____	is	on _____ Avenue. _____ Street.
		next to the _____. across from
		between the _____ and the _____.
		on the corner of _____ St. and _____ St.

Time*

A. Write the correct time under each clock.

seven o'clock	three o'clock	four thirty
six thirty	twelve o'clock	eleven thirty
nine thirty	two thirty	five o'clock
one o'clock	five thirty	eight thirty

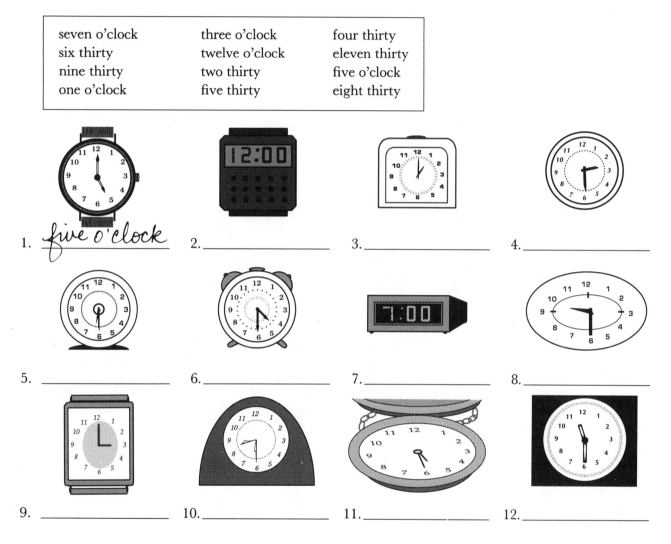

1. *five o'clock* 2. _____ 3. _____ 4. _____

5. _____ 6. _____ 7. _____ 8. _____

9. _____ 10. _____ 11. _____ 12. _____

B. Ask and answer questions about the time using the clocks above.

    Example: What time is it?
                It's five o'clock.

*See appendix for numbers.

C. Complete these sentences with any time.

    1. My class is at _____.

    2. My bus is at _____.

    3. My doctor's appointment is at _____.

    4. The bank is open at _____.

    5. The post office is open at _____.

D. Write the correct time under each clock.

three forty	three o'clock	three twenty
three fifteen	three forty-five	three fifty-five
three ten	three-oh-five	three thirty
three thirty-five	three fifty	three twenty-five

1. *Three o'clock*   2. _____   3. _____   4. _____

5. _____   6. _____   7. _____   8. _____

9. _____   10. _____   11. _____   12. _____

E. Ask and answer questions about the time with the clocks above.

    Example: What time is it?
                It's three o'clock.

F. Complete these sentences with any time.

1. We are in school from _____ to _____ .

2. Our break is from _____ to _____ .

3. The store is open from _____ to _____ .

4. The diner is open from _____ to _____ .

5. I am at work from _____ to _____ .

Writing

A. Circle the correct time for each clock.

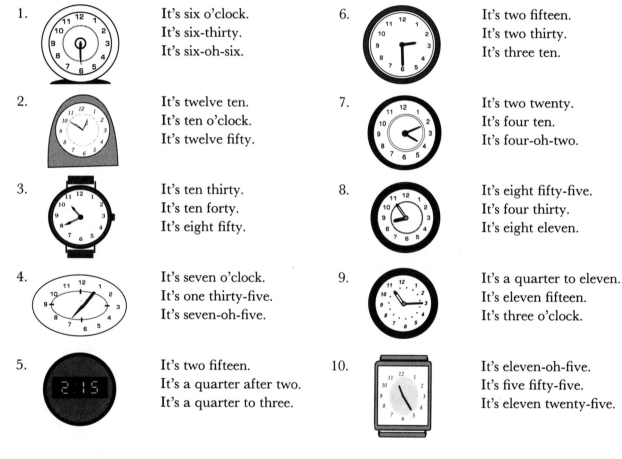

1. It's six o'clock.
   It's six-thirty.
   It's six-oh-six.

2. It's twelve ten.
   It's ten o'clock.
   It's twelve fifty.

3. It's ten thirty.
   It's ten forty.
   It's eight fifty.

4. It's seven o'clock.
   It's one thirty-five.
   It's seven-oh-five.

5. It's two fifteen.
   It's a quarter after two.
   It's a quarter to three.

6. It's two fifteen.
   It's two thirty.
   It's three ten.

7. It's two twenty.
   It's four ten.
   It's four-oh-two.

8. It's eight fifty-five.
   It's four thirty.
   It's eight eleven.

9. It's a quarter to eleven.
   It's eleven fifteen.
   It's three o'clock.

10. It's eleven-oh-five.
    It's five fifty-five.
    It's eleven twenty-five.

B. Put the correct time on these clocks.

It's nine thirty-five.

It's two-twenty.

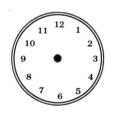

It's eleven fifteen.

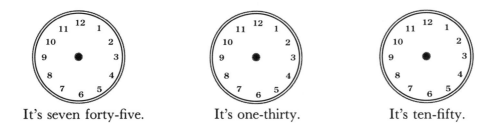

It's seven forty-five.   It's one-thirty.   It's ten-fifty.

C. Put a time on each clock. Write the question and answer.

Example:

What time is it?
It's seven fifteen.

1.

2.

3.

D. Fill in the conversations.

1. ___ ___ ___ ___ ___?
___ 11:00
oh, no. I'm late.

2. EXCUSE me.
___ ___ ___ ___?
sorry, I don't have a watch.

3.

4.

Grammar Summary

Time:

What time is it? .... It's 4:00 (four o'clock).
It's 4:15 (four fifteen).
It's 4:30 (four thirty).
It's 4:45 (four forty-five).

What time	is	it?

It	is	00:00.
		_____ o'clock.
		_____ fifteen.
		_____ thirty.
		_____ forty-five.

UNIT 11
A FAST FOOD RESTAURANT

Present Continuous Statements

A. Circle the actions of the people in the fast food restaurant.

walking	ordering	reading
talking	standing	eating
sleeping	working	playing
sitting	writing	drinking
running	cooking	cleaning
carrying	driving	paying

B. Answer these questions about the fast food restaurant.

> **Examples:** Who is taking orders from the customers?
> **Teresa is.**
> Who is working in back of the counter?
> **Teresa and Donna are.**

1. Who is ordering lunch?
2. Who is holding his mother's hand?
3. Who is standing in line and talking?
4. Who is standing at the end of the line?
5. Who is cooking in the kitchen?
6. Who is putting food on a tray?
7. Who is carrying a tray to a table?
8. Who is eating lunch with her children?
9. Who is sitting alone?
10. Who is cleaning tables?

C. These sentences are not true. Cross out the mistakes and say the sentence correctly.

> **Example:** Tommy is holding his ~~father~~'s hand.
> Tommy is holding his mother's hand.

1. Patty is paying for her breakfast.
2. Teresa is standing in front of the counter.
3. Michael is eating a hamburger.
4. Donna is putting food on a table.
5. Kim is eating lunch with her friend.
6. Ken and Ray are cooking chicken.
7. Mrs. Vo is talking to Olga.
8. Ali is carrying his tray to his car.
9. Michael is drinking a cup of coffee.
10. Bob is cleaning the floor.

D. Make true sentences about the fast food restaurant.

Patty Ali Michael Kim	is isn't	ordering eating cooking	lunch. a hamburger. hamburgers.
Ken and Ray Jason and Todd	are aren't	carrying drinking	a tray. soda.

Writing

A. Fill in the blank with the correct word.

is	isn't	are	aren't

1. Patty ___*isn't*___ ordering breakfast.

2. Teresa _____ standing in back of the counter.

3. Olga _____ standing with a friend.

4. Ken and Ray _____ taking orders from the customers.

5. Ali _____ sitting with Michael.

6. Kim _____ eating with her children.

7. Mr. and Mrs. Vo _____ sitting at a table.

8. Bob _____ washing the floor.

9. Michael _____ eating a big lunch.

10. Michael _____ only drinking a soda.

B. Write the verb in the present continuous tense.

1. Bob ___*is cleaning*___ (clean) tables.

2. Tommy _____ (stand) in line.

3. Jason and Todd _____ (eat) with their mother.

4. Patty _____ (order) a hamburger.

5. Teresa _____ (work) the lunch shift.

6. Ken and Ray _____ (work) in a hot kitchen.

7. Patty _____ (pay) for her lunch.

8. Donna _____ (put) soda on a tray.

9. Michael _____ (sit) at a table alone.

10. He _____ (drink) a soda.

C. Put the words in these sentences in order.

1. putting / Donna / on / is / . / food / tray / a

    Donna is putting food on a tray.

2. line / . / Mr. and Mrs. Vo / in / standing / are

    _____

3. hot / cooking / in / . / Ken and Ray / are / kitchen / the

    _____

4. paying for / Patty / lunch / . / is / her

    _____

5. lunch / children / . / Kim / eating / with / is / her

    _____

6. hamburgers / children / Kim's / eating / . / are

    _____

7. eating / Bob / . / lunch / isn't

    _____

8. ordering / . / Patty / big / is / lunch / a

    _____

9. isn't / friend / . / standing / Olga / with / a

    _____

10. are / . / people / Six / standing / in / line

    _____

D. Read the story. Then read each sentence. Circle "T" is the sentence is true, "F" if the sentence is false.

TERESA

Teresa is a counter clerk at Mr. Burger. This is her first day of work, and she is very nervous. Teresa is standing in back of the counter. Six customers are waiting in line. Patty is giving her order to Teresa, and Donna is putting the food on a tray. Teresa is ringing up Patty's order on the register. Patty's order is $3.50. She's paying with a $10 bill. Teresa is giving Patty $7.50 in change.

1. Teresa is a counter clerk.	Ⓣ	F
2. This is her first day of work.	T	F
3. Teresa is busy.	T	F
4. Five people are standing in line.	T	F
5. Teresa is cooking hamburgers for the customers.	T	F
6. Teresa is putting the orders on the trays.	T	F
7. Donna is ringing up the order on the register.	T	F
8. Patty's order is $2.50.	T	F
9. Patty is giving Teresa ten dollars.	T	F
10. Teresa is giving Patty the wrong change.	T	F

Grammar Summary

Present Continuous Statements:

Kim is eating (now).
She isn't cooking.
Ken and Ray are cooking.
They aren't eating.

I	am am not	
He/She/It	is isn't	verb + ing.
We/You/They	are aren't	

Present Continuous Yes / No Questions
Review of Possessive Adjectives

A. Circle the actions at break time in this school.

talking	combing	eating
drinking	washing	putting on
sleeping	running	smoking
fixing	sharpening	reading

B. Read each sentence about the picture and circle "Yes" or "No".

1. Kim is calling her son.   (Yes)   No
2. Paul is putting on his hat.   Yes   No
3. Teresa and Patty are doing their homework.   Yes   No
4. Mary is putting on her lipstick.   Yes   No
5. Ann is filing her nails.   Yes   No
6. Olga is washing her face.   Yes   No
7. Ellen and Susan are combing their hair.   Yes   No
8. Michael is drinking a cup of coffee.   Yes   No
9. David is smoking a cigarette.   Yes   No
10. Ali is sharpening his pencil.   Yes   No

C. Make true sentences about the picture.

Ann Ali Paul	is isn't	combing calling doing	his her	hair. son. homework.
Teresa and Patty Ellen and Susan	are aren't	putting on sharpening	their	sweater(s). pencil(s).

D. Answer these questions about the picture.

Yes, he is. No, he isn't.	Yes, she is. No, she isn't.	Yes, they are. No, they aren't.

1. Is Olga washing her face?
2. Are Mary and Ann combing their hair?
3. Is Paul putting on his coat?
4. Is Ali sharpening his pencil?
5. Are Teresa and Patty sitting in the cafeteria?
6. Are Teresa and Patty doing their homework?
7. Is Olga calling her son?
8. Is Harry fixing his tape recorder?
9. Is David eating an apple?
10. Are Ellen and Susan combing their hair?

Writing

A. Fill in each blank with the correct word.

his	her	their

1. Mary is putting on ___*her*___ lipstick.

2. Harry is fixing _____ tape recorder.

3. Ann is filing _____ nails.

4. Teresa and Patty are doing _____ homework.

5. Paul is putting on _____ sweater.

6. Ali is sharpening _____ pencil.

7. Olga is washing _____ hands.

8. Ellen and Susan are combing _____ hair.

9. Kim is calling _____ son.

10. Michael is drinking _____ soda.

B. Correct these sentences about break time.

1. Olga is washing her hair.

   Olga isn't washing her hair.
   She's washing her hands.

2. Paul is putting on his shirt.

   _____

   _____

3. Michael is drinking a cup of coffee.

   _____

   _____

4. Kim is calling her daughter.

_____

_____

5. Teresa and Patty are writing letters.

_____

_____

C. Put the words in these questions in order. Then, write the short answer.

1. Olga / Is / ? / her / washing / hands

Is Olga washing her hands?   _Yes, she is._

2. fixing / Harry / tape recorder / Is / ? / his

_____   _____

3. pencil / sharpening / Ali / Is / ? / his

_____   _____

4. doing / Michael / David / homework / their / Are / ? / and

_____   _____

5. Kim / her / ? / Is / combing / hair

_____   _____ .

D. Read this story. Then, write questions about the story.

BREAK TIME

It's break time. Break time is from 8:00 to 8:15 every night.

Some students are in the cafeteria. Kim is calling her son, Jason. He's home alone tonight. She's asking him, "Is everything all right?" Michael and David are sitting at a table and talking about baseball, their favorite sport.

Some students are in the ladies' room. Olga is washing her hands. Ellen and Susan are combing their hair. Ellen is saying to Susan, "Your new hair style is beautiful."

Some students are in the classroom. Teresa and Patty are doing their homework together. Teresa is helping Patty with some new work. Mary and Ann are sitting and talking. Mary is putting on her lipstick, and Ann is filing her nails. Her nails are very long. Every night, they're a different color. Ali and Harry are standing at the desk. Ali is sharpening his pencil. Harry is trying to fix his tape recorder. It isn't working. Ali is saying, "Maybe the batteries are dead."

1. *Is it break time?*

   Yes, it is. It's break time.

2. _____

   No, she isn't. Kim isn't calling her husband.

3. _____

   Yes, they are. David and Michael are talking about baseball.

4. _____

   Yes, she is. Olga is washing her hands.

5. _____

   No, they aren't. Ellen and Susan aren't washing their hair.

6. _____

   Yes, they are. Patty and Teresa are doing their homework.

7. _____

   Yes, she is. Teresa is helping Patty.

8. _____

   No, she isn't. Mary isn't putting on her sweater.

9. _____

   Yes, he is. Ali is sharpening his pencil.

10. _____

    No, they aren't. The batteries are dead.

Grammar Summary

Present Continuous Yes / No Questions

Are Harry and Ali talking? .... Yes, they are.
Is Paul talking? .... No, he isn't.

Am	I	
Is	he/she/it	verbing?
Are	we/you/they	

THE TRAIN STATION

Present Continuous Wh Questions

A. Circle the things that people are holding or carrying in the train station.

a ticket	a cup of coffee	a pocketbook
a briefcase	a bench	an umbrella
a donut	a newspaper	a handkerchief
a suitcase	a train schedule	a clock

B. Answer these questions about the train station.

Example: Who is buying a ticket at the ticket window?
Ali is.

1. Who is running for the train?
2. Who is carrying a briefcase?
3. Who is reading a newspaper and waiting for the train?
4. Who is collecting tickets?
5. Who is looking at the train schedule?
6. Who is eating a donut?
7. Who is drinking a cup of coffee?
8. Who is carrying a suitcase?
9. Who is giving a ticket to the conductor?
10. Who is crying and saying good-bye to her boyfriend?

C. Circle the correct answer.

1. What is Kim doing?
   a. Reading a newspaper.   b. A newspaper.
2. What is Kim reading?
   a. Reading a newspaper.   b. A newspaper.
3. What is Paul doing?
   a. Looking at a train schedule.   b. A train schedule.
4. What is Paul looking at?
   a. Looking at a train schedule.   b. A train schedule.
5. What is Sarah saying?
   a. Saying "Good-bye" to her boyfriend.   b. "Good-bye."
6. What is Sarah doing?
   a. Saying "Good-bye" to her boyfriend.   b. "Good-bye."
7. What are Ali and Lee doing?
   a. Buying tickets.   b. Tickets.
8. What are Ali and Lee buying?
   a. Buying tickets.   b. Tickets.
9. What is the conductor doing?
   a. Collecting tickets.   b. Tickets.
10. What is the conductor collecting?
    a. Collecting tickets.   b. Tickets.
11. What is Patty eating?
    a. Eating a donut.   b. A donut.
12. What is Patty doing?
    a. Eating a donut.   b. A donut.

D. Answer these questions about the train station.

1. Who is reading the newspaper?   Kim is.
2. What is Kim doing?
3. What is Kim reading?
4. Where is Kim sitting?
5. Who is looking at the clock?
6. What is Paul doing?
7. What is Paul holding in his hand?
8. Where is Paul sitting?
9. Who is running for the train?
10. What is Michael doing?
11. What is Michael carrying?
12. Who is drinking a cup of coffee?
13. Who is eating a donut?
14. What are Patty and Teresa doing?
15. Where are Patty and Teresa standing?

Writing

A. Put the words in these questions in order.

1. Kim / ? / doing / is / What

   What is Kim doing?

2. running / Who / for / is / ? / train / the

   _____

3. Ali / buying / What / ? / is

   _____

4. standing / ? / are / Patty / Where / Teresa / and

   _____

5. is / sitting / Where / Kim / ? /

   _____

6. / ? / drinking / is / cup / of / Who / a / coffee

   _____

7. Paul / looking at / ? / What / is

_____

8. doing / conductor / is / What / ? / the

_____

9. Lee / Where / ? / standing / is

_____

10. carrying / Michael / is / What / ?

_____

B. Fill in the blank with the correct word.

Who	What	Where

1. ___*Who*___ is buying a ticket?   Ali is.

2. _____ is Michael doing?   Running for the train.

3. _____ is carrying a briefcase?   David is.

4. _____ is Lee standing?   In line.

5. _____ is Sarah doing?   Saying good-bye.

6. _____ is Tom carrying?   His suitcases.

7. _____ is Paul doing?   Waiting for his train.

8. _____ is Paul sitting?   On a bench.

9. _____ are Teresa and Patty standing? In front of the donut stand.

10. _____ is Teresa drinking?   Coffee.

C. Use the chart and write ten questions about the train station. Then, answer the questions.

What	is	Ali Lee Kim Paul	doing? standing? buying? waiting for?
Where	are	Ali and Lee Kim and Paul	sitting?

1. _What is Ali doing?_   _Buying a ticket._
2. _____ _____
3. _____ _____
4. _____ _____
5. _____ _____
6. _____ _____
7. _____ _____
8. _____ _____
9. _____ _____
10. _____ _____

D. Read this story. Then, write the questions about the story.

GOOD-BYE

Sarah is standing next to the train. She's very sad. She's crying. She's waving to Tom, her boyfriend. She is unhappy because Tom is leaving. Tom is her boyfriend. He's getting on the train with his suitcases.

Sarah is 18 and she's in high school. Tom is 19 and he is going into the army. Tom is sad about Sarah, but he's excited about his future. He's saying, "Why are you crying?" Sarah is saying, "Because you're leaving and I'm sad." Tom is answering, "I'm not leaving forever. You're my girl."

1. Where _is Sarah standing_____?

Next to the train.

2. What _____?

She's crying.

3. Who _____?

Her boyfriend is.

4. What _____?

He's getting on the train.

5. Where _____?

Into the army.

6. Why _____?

Because Tom is leaving.

7. What _____?

"You're my girl."

Grammar Summary

Present Continuous Wh — Questions:

What is Kim doing? .... She's reading.
What is Kim reading? .... A newspaper.
Where is Kim reading? .... On a bench.

What	am	I	verbing?
Where	is	he/she/it	
	are	we/you/they	

Who is reading? . . . . Kim is.

Who	is	verbing?	.... I am.
			.... He/She/It is.
			.... We/You/They are.

*See appendix for spelling rules.

THE WEATHER

"What's the weather?"

1. _____

2. _____

3. _____

4. _____

5. _____

6. _____

A. What's the weather? Write the weather under each picture.

It's sunny.	It's raining.	It's snowing.
It's cloudy.	It's windy.	It's foggy.

B. What's the temperature?* Ask and answer questions about the temperature.

hot	warm	cool	cold	_____ ° (degrees)

Example: What's the temperature?

It's _cool_ .   It's _50°_ (fifty degrees)

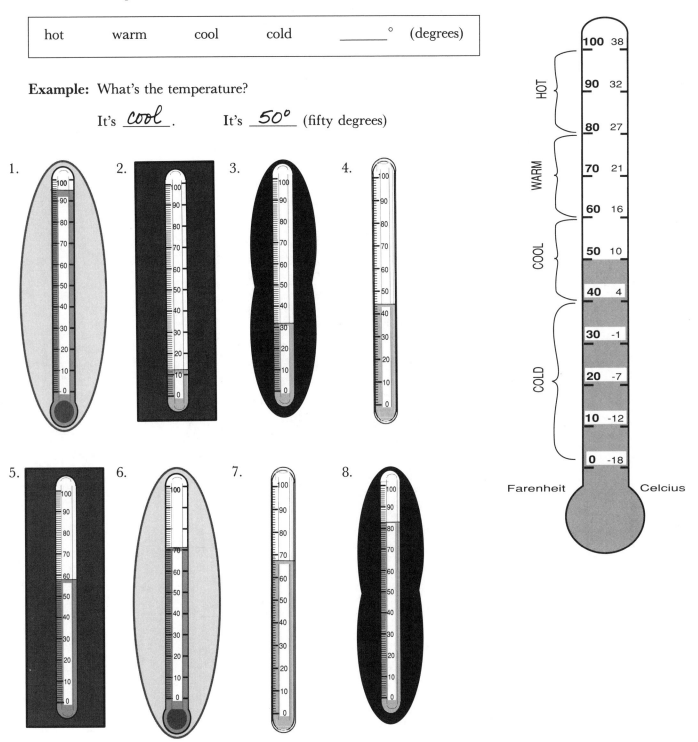

1.

2.

3.

4.

5.

6.

7.

8.

HOT

WARM

COOL

COLD

100	38
90	32
80	27
70	21
60	16
50	10
40	4
30	-1
20	-7
10	-12
0	-18

Farenheit   Celcius

C. Ask and answer these questions about each city on the weather map.

What's the weather in _____?	It's _____.
What's the temperature in _____?	It's _____. It's ___°.

Example: What's the weather in Houston? It's sunny.
What's the temperature? It's hot. It's 80°. (eighty degrees)

D. Answer these questions about the weather map.

1. Is it sunny in Miami?
2. What's the temperature in Miami?
3. What's the weather in Boston?
4. Is it cold in Boston today?
5. Is it raining in Denver?
6. What's the temperature there?
7. What's the weather in Los Angeles?
8. Is it sunny there today?
9. Is it hot or cold in Chicago today?
10. What's the weather in Chicago today?

*See appendix for numbers.

Writing

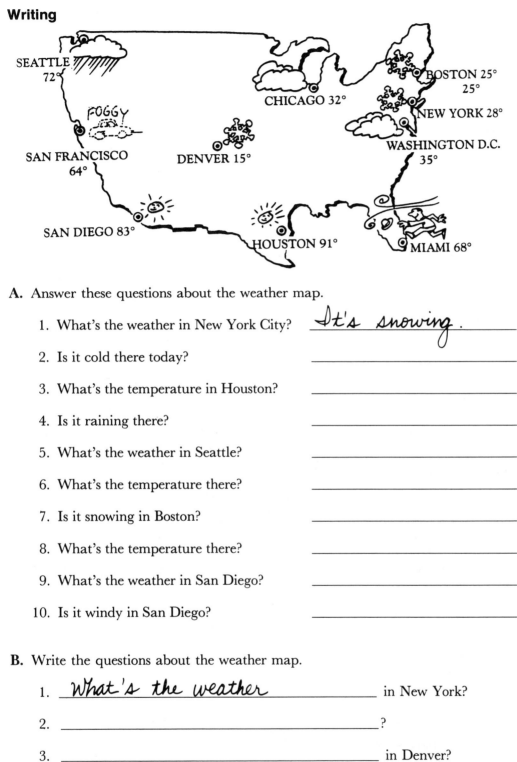

SEATTLE 72°

CHICAGO 32°

BOSTON 25° 25°

NEW YORK 28°

FOGGY

WASHINGTON D.C. 35°

SAN FRANCISCO 64°

DENVER 15°

SAN DIEGO 83°

HOUSTON 91°

MIAMI 68°

A. Answer these questions about the weather map.

1. What's the weather in New York City? *It's snowing.*

2. Is it cold there today? _____

3. What's the temperature in Houston? _____

4. Is it raining there? _____

5. What's the weather in Seattle? _____

6. What's the temperature there? _____

7. Is it snowing in Boston? _____

8. What's the temperature there? _____

9. What's the weather in San Diego? _____

10. Is it windy in San Diego? _____

B. Write the questions about the weather map.

1. *What's the weather* _____ in New York?   It's snowing.

2. _____? Yes, it is.

3. _____ in Denver? It's 15°.

4. _____? It's snowing.

5. _____ in Boston? No, it isn't.

6. _____ in Boston? It's 25°.

7. _____ in Miami?   It's 68°.

8. _____ ?   It's cloudy.

9. _____ in San Francisco?   It's foggy.

10. _____ ?   It's 64°.

C. Answer these questions about the weather in your area.

1. What's the weather today? _____   2. Is it sunny? _____

3. Is it windy? _____   4. Is it raining? _____

5. What's the temperature? _____

D. Fill in these conversations.

1.

2.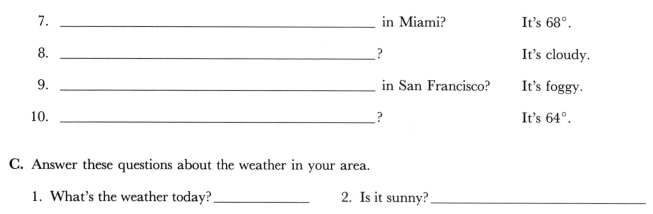

3.

4.

Grammar Summary

Weather:

What's the weather in Washington? . . . . It's cloudy and cold.
What's the temperature in Miami? . . . . It's hot. It's 90° (ninety degrees).

What	is	the weather the temperature	?
		It	is _____ and _____ .
			_____ (degrees).

THE PARK

There is / are Statements and Yes / No Questions

A. Circle the items you see in the park.

water fountain	picnic table	bathrooms
river	barbecue grill	snack bar
ducks	swings	pond
public telephone	sand box	benches
tennis courts	pool	boats for rent
basketball courts	statue	stadium

B. Read each statement about the park. Circle "Yes" or "No."

1. There is a pond in the park.   (Yes)   No
2. There is a pool in the park.   Yes   No
3. There are boats for rent on the pond.   Yes   No
4. There are some picnic tables in the park.   Yes   No
5. There are barbecue grills next to the pond.   Yes   No
6. There is a play area for children.   Yes   No
7. There are some swings in the play area.   Yes   No
8. There is a water fountain next to the tennis courts.   Yes   No
9. There are five basketball courts in the park.   Yes   No
10. There are benches around the pond.   Yes   No

C. Use this chart and make sentences about the park.

There	is a	water fountain pond play area sand box	in the park.
	are some	tennis courts boats for rent swings benches	

D. Answer these questions about the park.

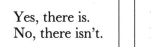

Yes, there is.	Yes, there are.
No, there isn't.	No, there aren't.

1. Is there a play area in the park?
2. Are there any tennis courts in the park?
3. Is there a flower garden in the park?
4. Is there an ice cream stand in the park?
5. Are there any swings in the play area?
6. Are there any benches around the pond?
7. Are there any public telephones in the park?
8. Are there any basketball courts in the park?
9. Is there a water fountain in the park?
10. Is there a pool in the park?

A. Write ten sentences about the pool.

1. *There are seven people in the pool.*
2. *There's a diving board on the right.*
3. _____
4. _____
5. _____
6. _____
7. _____
8. _____
9. _____
10. _____

B. Put the words in these questions in order. Then, write the short answer.

1. trees / any / Are / next to / pool / ? / there / the

   Are there any trees next to the pool?   _No, there aren't._

2. diving board / pool / Is / ? / a / there / at / this

   _____   _____

3. ? / pool / bathrooms / Are / any / the / at / there

   _____   _____

4. snack bar / ? / Is / pool / at / there / a / the

   _____   _____

5. children / ? / play area / there / Is / a / for

   _____   _____

6. around / benches / there / the / pool / ? / Are / any

   _____   _____

7. snack bar / Is / water fountain / ? / there / next to / a / the

   _____   _____

8. picnic tables / there / any / Are / pool / at / the

   _____   _____

9. pool / ? / barbecue grills / there / any / Are / at / the

   _____   _____

10. people / Are / many / pool / in / the / there / ?

   _____   _____

C. Ellen is new in town. She's asking about the community pool. Ann is answering her. Fill in their conversation.

1. _Are there any picnic tables at the pool_ ?

   Yes, _there are_ some picnic tables.

2. _____?

   Yes, _____ a good snack bar.

3. _____?

   No, _____ .

4. _____?

   Yes, _____ always a lifeguard.

5. _____?

   No, _____ .

6. _____?

   Yes, _____ . And it's very high.

7. _____?

   Yes, _____ a big baby pool.

8. _____?

   No, _____ .

Grammar Summary

There is / There are Affirmative Statements:

There is a pond in the park.
There are boats on the pond.
There are some picnic tables in the park.

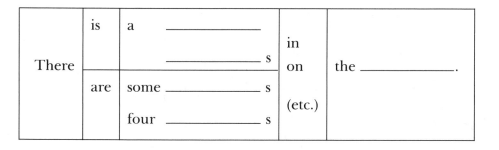

There is / There are Yes / No Questions and Short Answers:

Is there a pond in the park? . . . . Yes, there is.
Is there a statue in the park? . . . . No, there isn't.
Are there any boats in the park? . . . . Yes, there are.
Are there any telephones in the park? . . . . No, there aren't.

Is	there	a _____ _____	in on (etc.)	the _____?
Are		any _____ s		

The non-count question is:

Is	there	any	rice flour _____	in on (etc.)	the _____?

Note: We say, "The bank is on Park Avenue.", but
"There is <u>a</u> bank on Park Avenue.
We say, "The donuts are on the table.", but
"There are <u>some</u> donuts on the table."

Count and Non-Count Nouns

A. Circle the names of the food in this kitchen.

cereal	sugar	a lemon	ketchup
apples	spaghetti	oranges	corn
a cake	mayonnaise	bananas	carrots
flour	eggs	a pie	a turkey
donuts	margarine	ice cream	bread
cookies	rice	a pineapple	
lettuce	tomatoes	Italian dressing	

B. Look at the box above and write the name of each food in the correct column.

Singular Count	Plural Count	Non-count
a cake	apples	cereal

C. Use this chart and make sentences about the food in this kitchen.

There	is	a	pie lemon pineapple	in the refrigerator.
		some	ice cream bread cereal rice	in the freezer. in the cabinet.
	are	some	eggs oranges donuts bananas	on the counter.

D. What food comes in each container?

onions	mayonnaise	potato chips
soup	coffee	peanut butter
cereal	juice	
soy sauce	spaghetti	

box   bottle   can   bag   jar

cereal   _soy sauce_   _____   _____   _____

_____   _____   _____   _____   _____

E. Identify each picture.

Examples:

a bag of onions   a bottle of soda

1.

2.

3.

4.

5.

6.

7.

8.

9.

10.

11.

12.

Writing

A. Circle the name of the picture. Two answers are correct.

1. (some tuna) (two cans of tuna) some tunas two cans of tunas

2. some onion a bag of onion some onions a bag of onions

3. some oil three bottles of oil some oils three bottles of oils

4. some cookie two boxes of cookie some cookies two boxes of cookies

5. some jelly a jar of jelly some jellies a jar of jellies

6. some soup four cans of soup some soups four cans of soups

7. some potato two bags of potato some potatoes two bags of potatoes

8. some ketchup two bottles of ketchup some ketchups two bottles of ketchups

9. some rice a bag of rice some rices two bags of rice

10. some donut a box of donut some donuts a box of donuts

B. Fill in the blank with the correct word.

is	are	some

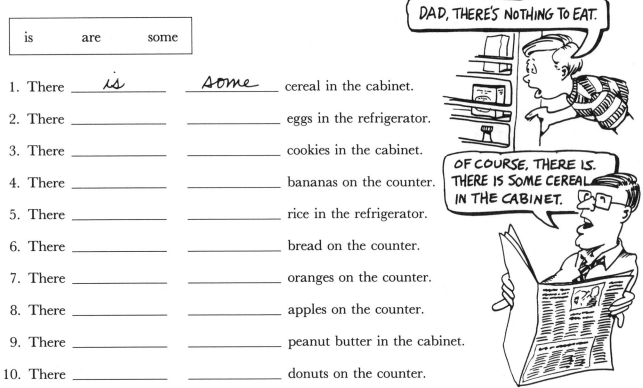

1. There ___is___ ___some___ cereal in the cabinet.

2. There _____ _____ eggs in the refrigerator.

3. There _____ _____ cookies in the cabinet.

4. There _____ _____ bananas on the counter.

5. There _____ _____ rice in the refrigerator.

6. There _____ _____ bread on the counter.

7. There _____ _____ oranges on the counter.

8. There _____ _____ apples on the counter.

9. There _____ _____ peanut butter in the cabinet.

10. There _____ _____ donuts on the counter.

C. Mrs. Gibson is at the check-out counter in the supermarket. Write ten sentences about the food she is buying.

1. ___She's buying a can of coffee___

2. _____

3. _____

90

4. _____

5. _____

6. _____

7. _____

8. _____

9. _____

10. _____

D. Write seven sentences about the food in your kitchen.

Example: There's a bottle of soda in my refrigerator.

1. _____

2. _____

3. _____

4. _____

5. _____

6. _____

7. _____

Grammar Summary

There is / There are with Count and Non-Count Nouns

1. Count nouns are things we can count: a donut, 2 donuts, 3 donuts, etc.
   Non-count nouns are things we can't count. We can measure them, but we can't say, "A rice, 2 rices, 3 rices, etc."
2. We can put things in containers, and can count the containers:
   a box of donuts, 2 boxes of donuts, etc.
   a bag of rice, 2 bags of rice, 3 bags of rice, etc.

There is Statements:

There is a lemon in the refrigerator. . . . . count
There is some rice in the cabinet. . . . . non-count
There is a box of rice in the cabinet. . . . . container of non-count
There is a bag of cookies on the counter. . . . . . . container of count

| There | is | a   count
some non-count

a container   of non-count

a container   of counts | in
on

(etc.) | the_____ . |

There are Statements:

There are some donuts on the counter. . . . . count
There are two boxes of donuts on the counter . . . . containers of count
There are some cans of soup in the cabinet . . . . . containers of non-count

| There | are | some counts
four counts
some   containers of counts
ten   containers of counts
some   containers of non-count
five   containers of non-count | in
on
(etc.) | the _____ . |

Going to Future Statements

A. Circle the things that people are bringing to the beach.

book	beach umbrella	newspaper
shovel	cooler	surfboard
frisbee	fishing rod	sunglasses
grill	beach chairs	blanket
ball	towels	

B. Answer these questions about the picture.

Example: Who is going to fish? Ali is.
               Who is going to swim? Everyone is.

1. Who is going to play ball?
2. Who is going to listen to the radio?
3. Who is going to cook hamburgers?
4. Who is going to read the newspaper?
5. Who is going to surf?
6. Who is going to lie in the sun?
7. Who is going to have a picnic lunch?
8. Who is going to swim?
9. Who is going to play frisbee?
10. Who is going to have a good time?

C. Use this chart and make true sentences about the picture.

Ali Patty Michael	is isn't	going to	play ball. surf. swim. read the newspaper.
Kim and Don Jason and Todd	are aren't		fish. cook the hamburgers.

D. Read each sentence. Circle "N" if the action is happening <u>now</u>. Circle "F" if the action is going to happen in the <u>future</u>.

	Now	Future
1. Patty is wearing sunglasses.	(N)	F
2. Ali is going to fish.	N	F
3. Michael is going to surf.	N	F
4. Patty is going to listen to the radio.	N	F
5. Todd is kicking the ball	N	F
6. Don and Kim are carrying the grill.	N	F
7. Don is going to cook the hamburgers.	N	F
8. Everyone is going to have a picnic lunch.	N	F
9. Patty is going to lie in the sun.	N	F
10. The people are walking to the beach.	N	F

Writing

A. Write the verb in the future tense.

1. These friends _are going to stay_ (stay) at the beach all day.

2. They _____ (lie) on the sand.

3. Ali _____ (fish) this afternoon.

4. Patty _____ (listen) to the radio.

5. The boys _____ (play) ball.

6. Don _____ (cook) hamburgers.

7. Everyone _____ (have) a picnic lunch.

8. They _____ (eat) a lot of food.

9. They _____ (enjoy) their day at the beach.

10. It _____ (be) sunny and hot all day.

B. Correct these sentences.

1. Patty is going to watch TV.

Patty isn't going to watch TV.
She's going to listen to the radio.

2. The boys are going to play basketball.

_____

_____

3. Don and Kim are going to cook chicken.

_____

_____

4. Michael is going to sail all day.

_____

_____

5. It's going to rain.

_____

_____

6. Ali is going to read a book.

_____

_____

7. The boys are going to swim in the pool.

_____

_____

C. Some friends at school are planning a family barbecue in the park for next weekend. These people are thinking about the barbecue. What is each person going to do?

play baseball	dance
wax his car	sit in the sun and relax
cook the chicken	look at the flower garden
rent a boat	take a long walk
help Lee	play tennis

1. *Olga is going to sit in the sun and relax.*

2. _____

3. _____

4. _____

5. _____

6. _____

7. _____

8. _____

9. _____

10. _____

Grammar Summary

Going to Future Affirmative and Negative:

Patty is going to listen to the radio.
He isn't going to cook.
Everyone is going to eat.
Don and Kim are not going to surf.
The boys are going to play ball.

I	am am not	
He/She/It	is isn't	going to <u>verb</u> .
We/You/They	are aren't	

A BUSY WEEKEND

Going to Future Yes / No Questions
It / Them

A. It's Saturday. Everyone is going to help with the housework. What is each person going to do? Look at the picture to find the answer.

✓ pay the bills	change her sheets	wash the windows
✓ wash the car	wash the dishes	water the plants
clean his room	wash the floor	dust the furniture
cut the grass	clean her room	fix the faucet
iron the shirts	wash the clothes	vacuum the rugs
go food shopping	change his sheets	

Examples: Olga is going to pay the bills.
David is going to wash the car.

B. Answer these questions about the housework this weekend.

Yes, he is.	Yes, she is.	Yes, they are.
No, he isn't.	No, she isn't.	No, they aren't.

1. Is Olga going to wash the windows?
2. Are Jeff and Kathy going to wash the car?
3. Is Jeff going to cut the grass?
4. Are Jeff and Kathy going to clean their rooms?
5. Is Olga going to iron the shirts?
6. Is Kathy going to dust the furniture?
7. Is David going to fix the faucet?
8. Are Kathy and Jeff going to water the plants?
9. Is Kathy going to wash the floor?
10. Is David going to wash the dishes?

C. Use this chart, and ask and answer questions about this family's plans. Answer the questions with short answers.

Is	Olga David Kathy Jeff	going to	wash vacuum clean change	the windows? the dishes? the car? the rugs? the rooms?
Are	Kathy and Jeff			the sheets?

D. Who's going to do each chore? Use "it" or "them" in the answer.

    Examples: The car is dirty.   David is going to wash it.
                  The clothes are dirty.   David is going to wash them.

1. The car is dirty.
2. The clothes are dirty.
3. The plants are dry.
4. The rugs are dirty.
5. The faucet is leaking.
6. The furniture is dusty.
7. The grass is high.
8. The bills are due.
9. Kathy's room is messy.
10. The dishes are dirty.

Writing

A. Look at the picture and answer these questions.

1. Is David going to wash the clothes?   _Yes, he is._

2. Is Kathy going to wash the dishes?   _____

3. Is Olga going to dust the furniture?   _____

4. Are Jeff and Kathy going to clean their rooms?   _____

5. Is Jeff going to cut the grass?   _____

6. Are David and Olga going to wash the windows?   _____

7. Is Kathy going to change her sheets?   _____

8. Is David going to vacuum the rugs?   _____

9. Is Olga going to water the plants?   _____

10. Are Kathy and Jeff going to help today?   _____

B. Fill in the blanks with words from the box below.

it	soon
them	later
	tomorrow

1. The floor is dirty. Olga is going to wash _it_ _later_

2. The plants are dry. Olga is going to water _them_ _soon._

3. The dishes are dirty. Kathy is going to wash _____ _____.

4. The faucet is leaking. David is going to fix _____ _____.

5. The furniture is dusty. Kathy is going to dust _____ _____.

6. The grass is high. David is going to cut _____ _____.

7. The bills are due. Olga is going to pay _____ _____.

8. Jeff's room is messy. He is going to clean _____ _____.

9. The rugs are dirty. Jeff is going to vacuum _____ _____.

10. The windows are dirty. Jeff is going to wash _____ _____.

C. Put the words in these questions in order. Then, write the short answer.

1. David / car / to / ? / going / Is / wash / the

   Is David going to wash the car?   _Yes, he is._

2. grass / the / ? / Olga / Is / cut / to / going

   _____   _____

3. to / room / Kathy / Is / ? / going / clean / her

   _____   _____

4. dishes / ? / going / wash / to / Jeff / the / Is

   _____   _____

5. food / going / go / shopping / David / ? / Is / to

   _____   _____

6. shirts / Olga / ? / to / the / iron / Is / going

   _____   _____

7. Is / ? / faucet / Kathy / going / the / fix / to

   _____   _____

8. windows / Jeff / ? / the / to / Is / going / wash

   _____   _____

9. Kathy / going / ? / Are / to / Jeff / bills / pay / the / and

   _____   _____

10. clothes / David / to / wash / Is / going / ? / the

   _____   _____

D. Read the story. Then, answer the questions.

THE BEAL FAMILY

It's Saturday evening and everyone in the Beal family is tired. The house is beautiful; everything is clean and in order. Olga is saying, "That's it for me! I'm tired. I'm not going to cook tonight."

David is laughing. "I agree. Let's go to Gino's." So, they are all going to eat out at an Italian restaurant near their house. Everyone is going to order his favorite food. The children are going to order pizza with sausage and onions. Olga is going to order spaghetti and meatballs, and David is going to order lasagna.

After dinner, they are going to stop at the video store and pick out some movies. They are probably going to rent a science fiction movie for the children and a comedy for David and Olga.

Answer these questions about the story.

1. Are the Beals going to do more housework?

   No, they aren't.

2. Why not?

   _____

3. Is Olga going to cook tonight?

   _____

4. Why not?

   _____

5. Is Gino's an Italian restaurant or a friend's house?

   _____

6. Are the Beals going to eat at a French restaurant?

   _____

7. Are the children going to order pizza?

   _____

8. Is David going to order pizza?

   _____

9. Are the Beals going to go to the movies?

_____

10. Are they going to rent some movies?

_____

11. Are the children going to watch a comedy?

_____

12. Are the Beals going to relax tonight?

_____

Grammar Summary

Going to Future Yes / No Questions:

Is Jeff going to wash the car? No, he isn't.
Jeff's not going to wash the car.
David is going to wash it.
Are the children going to wash the clothes? No, they aren't.
The children aren't going to wash the clothes.
David is going to wash them.

Am	I			going to <u>verb</u>	the _____ ?
Is	he/she/it				the _____ s?
Are	we/you/they				
	I	am am not		going to <u>verb</u>	the _____ it.
	He/She/It	is isn't			the _____.
	We/You/They	are aren't			them.

Going to Future Wh Questions

Person: Teresa
Place:
Transportation:
Dates:

Person: David and his family
Place:
Transportation:
Dates:

Los Angeles

Chicago

Person: Michael
Place:
Transportation:
Dates:

Washington, D.C.

florida

Person: Ali and his friend
Place:
Transportation:
Dates:

A. Read the sentences. Then, fill in the boxes on the map.

1. Michael is going to drive to Washington, D.C., on August 3.
2. He's only going to stay there for the weekend.
3. Ali is going to take a vacation with a friend.
4. They are going to fly to Orlando.
5. They are going to arrive on August 10 and stay for one week.
6. David is going to drive to Los Angeles with his wife and children.
7. They're going to leave on June 20.
8. They're going to travel and camp out for a month.
9. Teresa is going to take the train to Chicago on July 1.
10. She's going to stay with her sister for ten days.

B. Answer these yes/no questions about everybody's vacation plans.

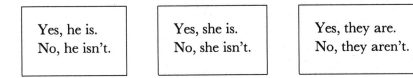

| Yes, he is. | Yes, she is. | Yes, they are. |
| No, he isn't. | No, she isn't. | No, they aren't. |

1. Is Michael going to fly to Washington, D.C.?
2. Is he going to travel alone?
3. Is he going to stay for one week?
4. Is Ali going to stay in Orlando for a week?
5. Is Ali going to go by plane?
6. Is his friend going to travel with him?
7. Are David and his family going to drive to Los Angeles?
8. Are they going to stay in a motel every night?
9. Are they going to cook out?
10. Is Teresa going to visit her sister?
11. Is she going to stay for two weeks?

C. Answer these questions about the information on the map.

1. Where is Teresa going to go?
2. What is she going to do there?
3. When is she going to leave?
4. When is she going to return?
5. How long is she going to stay?
6. Where are David and his family going to go?
7. What are they going to do?
8. When are they going to leave?
9. When are they going to return?
10. How long are they going to stay?

D. Ask questions about each person's vacation plans. Then, answer the questions.

Where	is	Ali Teresa Michael	going to	go? leave?
When		David and his family		stay?
What	are	Ali and his friend		do?

Writing

A. Put the words in these questions in order. Then, write the short answer.

1. visit / going / ? / Is / brother / Teresa / to / her

   Is Teresa going to visit her brother ?   *No, she isn't.*

2. Is / take / to / she / ? / going / the / train

   _____?   _____

3. on / ? / she / return / Is / going / July 1 / to

   _____?   _____

4. July 11 / she / going / Is / ? / leave / on / to

   _____?   _____

5. stay / two / Is / going / ? / she / to / weeks / for

   _____?   _____

6. Los Angeles / David and his family / Are / drive / ? / to / going / to

   _____?   _____

7. a / camper / going / ? / travel / Are / to / in / they

   _____?   _____

8. long / take / Are / going / to / they / vacation / ? / a

   _____?   _____

9. return / June 20 / Are / ? / they / to / going / on

   _____?   _____

10. the / country / they / ? / Are / see / going / a lot of / to

    _____?   _____

B. Write questions about Michael's vacation plans.

1. Where _*is Michael going to go*_____? To Washington, D.C.

2. How long _____? For three days.

3. What _____? Visit the White House.

4. When _____? On August 3.

5. When _____? On August 5.

Write questions about Ali and his friend's vacation plans.

6. Where *are Ali and his friend going to go* ? To Orlando.

7. What _____? See Disney World.

8. When _____? On August 10.

9. When _____? On August 17.

10. How long _____? For one week.

C. Choose a place on this map. Imagine you are going to visit this area. Answer these questions about your plans.

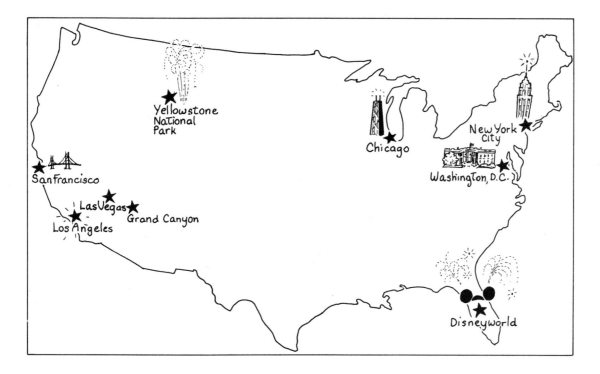

1. Where are you going to go?

   I'm _____

2. Who are you going to go with?

   _____

3. What are you going to do during the day?

   _____

4. What are you going to do at night?

   _____

5. Where are you going to stay?

   _____

6. When are you going to leave?

   _____

7. When are you going to return?

   _____

8. How long are you going to stay there?

   _____

9. Is this going to be your first visit to _____ ?

   _____

Grammar Summary

Going to Future Wh Questions:

What is Teresa going to do? . . . . Visit her family.
Where is she going to go? . . . . To Chicago.
When is she going to leave? . . . . On July 1.
When is she going to return? . . . . On July 11.
How long is she going to stay? . . . . For 10 days.

What Where When How long	am	I	going to	verb ?
	is	he/she/it		
	are	we/you/they		

108

A TYPICAL DAY

Simple Present Statements

A. Look at Susan's and Paul's daily routine. Fill in each blank with the correct time.

1. They get up at **7:00**.

2. They eat breakfast at _____.

3. Susan walks to work at _____.

4. Paul works from _____ to _____.

5. They eat dinner at _____.

6. Susan studies nursing from _____ to _____.

7. Paul's computer class starts at _____.

8. Susan reads from _____ to _____.

9. Paul watches TV from _____ to _____.

10. They go to bed at _____.

B. These sentences are not true. Cross out the mistakes and say the sentences correctly.

Example: Susan drinks ~~coffee~~ in the morning.
Susan drinks tea in the morning.

1. Susan and Paul get up at 8:00.
2. They eat breakfast at 7:00.
3. Paul drinks tea for breakfast.
4. Susan drives to work.
5. Paul works from 9:00 to 4:00.
6. They eat dinner at 7:00.
7. Susan studies typing.
8. After class, Susan watches TV.
9. After class, Paul studies.
10. They go to bed at 11:00.

C. Circle the correct verb in each sentence.

1. She **get up** (**gets up**) at 7:00.
2. They **eat** **eats** breakfast at 7:30.
3. He **drink** **drinks** coffee.
4. They **leave** **leaves** for work at 8:00.
5. She **walk** **walks** to work.
6. She **work** **works** from 9:00 to 5:00.
7. They **go** **goes** to school in the evening.
8. They **get** **gets** home from school at 10:00.
9. He **watch** **watches** TV after school.
10. They **go** **goes** to sleep at 12:00.

D. Make true sentences about Susan and Paul.

Susan Paul	gets up works goes to school gets home	at 7:00. from 9:00 to 5:00.
Susan and Paul	get up work go to school get home	from 7:00 to 9:30. at 10:00

110

E. Look at the pictures and make sentences about Susan's and Paul's day.

Example: Paul eats breakfast at 7:30. **or**
Susan eats breakfast at 7:30. **or**
They eat breakfast at 7:30.

Writing

A. Write ten true sentences about Susan's and Paul's daily routine.

Susan Paul	goes studies has	to work. to school.
Susan and Paul	go study have	in the evening. at a community college. a busy week.

1. *Susan goes to school.*

2. _____

3. _____

4. _____

5. _____

6. _____

7. _____

8. _____

9. _____

10. _____

B. Write the correct form of the verb in the present tense.

1. Susan _____*gets up*_____ (get up) at 7:00.

2. She _____ (eat) breakfast with her husband.

3. Susan _____ (drink) tea, and her husband _____ (drink) coffee.

4. They _____ (leave) for work at 8:00.

5. Paul _____ (drive) to work; Susan _____ (walk).

6. They _____ (work) from 9:00 to 5:00.

7. After work, they _____ (eat) dinner.

8. Susan and Paul _____ (study) at night.

9. After school, Susan _____ (read) and Paul _____ (watch) TV.

10. They _____ (go) to bed at 12:00.

C. Read the story.

A TYPICAL DAY

Susan and Paul (are) a young, married couple. They (have) a busy week. They both get up at 7:00 in the morning. At 7:30, they eat a small breakfast, usually toast and juice. Susan drinks tea; Paul drinks coffee. At 8:00 they leave for work. Susan walks to work because she lives near her office. Paul drives to work because he lives 15 miles from his company. They both work from 9:00 to 5:00, and they get home at about 5:30. They cook dinner together and eat at about 6:00. Then, they go to school. They take their books and drive to a community college in their area. Susan studies nursing, and Paul studies computer science. They arrive home at 10:00. It's a long day, and they are tired. They talk and relax. Sometimes they study. Sometimes Susan reads and Paul watches TV. At 12:00, they go to bed.

D. Circle the verbs in the story above. Then, write ten sentences about your daily routine. Use verbs from the story.

Example: _____*I get up at 6:30 in the morning.*_____

1. _____

2. _____

3. _____

4. _____

5. _____

6. _____

7. _____

8. _____

9. _____

10. _____

Grammar Summary

The Simple Present Tense

The verb talks about routine actions. These happen every day, every weekend, every week, etc.

Simple Present Affirmative Statements:

Susan walks to work.
Paul drives to work.
They work from 9:00 to 5:00.
They eat dinner at 6:00.

I We/You/They	verb	(from 00:00 to 00:00). (at 00:00).
He/She/It	verb**s**	

MORNING

Simple Present Negatives and Yes / No Questions

A. Read these sentences about the people in this apartment building. Circle "Yes" or "No."

1. Michael lives on the third floor.   (Yes)   No
2. He lives alone.   Yes   No
3. Michael takes the bus to work.   Yes   No
4. Susan and Paul live on the first floor.   Yes   No
5. Paul drives to work.   Yes   No
6. Paul drives Susan to work.   Yes   No
7. Kim and Don live on the first floor.   Yes   No
8. Don drives to work.   Yes   No
9. The boys take the bus to school.   Yes   No
10. Everyone leaves at the same time.   Yes   No

B. Answer these questions about the people in this building.

| Yes, s/he does. |
| No, s/he doesn't. |

| Yes, they do. |
| No, they don't. |

   1. Does Michael live with his family?
   2. Does he work?
   3. Does Michael wear a suit to work?
   4. Do Susan and Paul live on the second floor?
   5. Does Paul wear a suit to work?
   6. Does Susan walk to work?
   7. Do Kim and Don live on the first floor?
   8. Do the boys take the bus to school?
   9. Does Kim drive Don to work?
10. Does Kim stay home?

C. Use the chart and make true statements about the people in this building.

Michael Susan	lives doesn't live walks doesn't walk	alone. on the first floor. on the second floor.
The boys	live don't live walk don't walk	on the third floor. to work. to school.

D. These sentences are not true. Cross out the mistakes and say the sentences correctly.

Example: Michael lives on the ~~second~~ floor.
              Michael doesn't live on the second floor.
              He lives on the third floor.

   1. Michael lives on the first floor.
   2. Michael lives with his family.
   3. Michael wears jeans to work.
   4. Susan and Paul live on the third floor.
   5. Susan and Paul have two children.
   6. Susan drives to work.
   7. Don and Kim live on the second floor.
   8. Don and Kim have two girls.
   9. Don drives to work.
10. The boys take the bus to school.

Writing

A. Circle the correct negative verb in each sentence.

1. Michael   (doesn't live)   don't live   with his family.
2. Michael   doesn't stay   don't stay   home all day.
3. Michael   doesn't take   don't take   the bus to work.
4. Susan and Paul doesn't live   don't live   on the first floor.
5. Susan   doesn't drive   don't drive   to work.
6. Susan and Paul doesn't have   don't have   any children.
7. Kim and Don   doesn't live   don't live   in a house.
8. Their boys   doesn't take   don't take   the bus to school.
9. Kim   doesn't drive   don't drive   the boys to school.
10. Kim   doesn't go   don't go   to work.

B. Put these questions in the correct order. Then, write the short answer.

1. Don / bus / work / to / Does / ? / the / take

   Does Don take the bus to work?   _Yes, he does._

2. wear / ? / suit / a / Does / Paul / work / to

   _____   _____

3. Michael / Does / ? / alone / live

   _____   _____

4. together / Michael / Don / and / Do / ? / drive

   _____   _____

5. Do / to / school / ? / the / take / the / bus / boys

   _____   _____

6. ? / work / Susan / Does / her / house / near

   _____   _____

7. have / Kim / children / and / four / ? / Do / Don

   _____   _____

8. the / ? / the / third / boys / live / Do / floor / on

   _____   _____

9. stay / Kim / ? / home / Does

   _____   _____

10. jeans / boys / ? / school / Do / wear / to / the

    _____   _____

C. Use the chart and write ten questions about the people in the apartment building. Then, write short answers.

Does	Michael Susan Don	walk drive take the bus	to work?
Do	the boys	wear a suit wear jeans	to school?

1. *Does Michael take the bus to work?*   *No, he doesn't.*

2. _____   _____

3. _____   _____

4. _____   _____

5. _____   _____

6. _____   _____

7. _____   _____

8. _____   _____

9. _____   _____

10. _____   _____

D. Read the story. Then, answer the questions.

THE APARTMENT BUILDING

Kim lives on the first floor of this building on Broad Street. It's a noisy building from 7:00 to 8:00 every morning because everybody is getting ready for work.

Michael lives alone in the big apartment on the third floor. He's single, and he goes to parties every night, so he wakes up late every morning. He drives to work at 8:00, but he's always late and always in a hurry. His feet make noise on the stairs.

Susan and Paul are a young married couple. They live on the second floor. They leave at 8:00 a.m., too. Susan is a secretary in a small office near her apartment. She walks to work and enjoys the exercise. Paul works in a factory about fifteen miles from their home. He drives the car.

Kim and Don live on the first floor with their two sons, Jason and Todd. They have a car, but Don takes the bus to work. His office is only a fifteen-minute bus ride away. Jason and Todd walk to school together. Kim waves good-bye to them.

At 8:00, everything is quiet. Kim is alone. She has peace and quiet. Now, she can draw and paint. Kim is an artist.

1. Does Michael have a small apartment?   *No, he doesn't.*

2. Does he stay home at night?   _____

3. Do Susan and Paul leave at the same time?   _____

4. Does Susan like to walk to work?   _____

5. Does Paul live near his factory?   _____

6. Do Kim and Don have a car?   _____

7. Does Kim drive the boys to school every day?   _____

8. Do the boys leave at 8:00 in the morning?   _____

9. Does Kim work?   _____

10. Does she walk to work?   _____

Grammar Summary

Simple Present Negative Statements:

Susan doesn't drive to work.
Paul doesn't walk to work.
The boys don't drive to school.

I			
	don't	verb	
We/You/They			_____ .
He/She/It	doesn't		

Simple Present Yes / No Questions and Short Answers:

Does Michael live on the first floor? . . . . No, he doesn't.
Do the boys live on the first floor? . . . . Yes, they do.

Do	I we/you/they	verb	_____ ?
Does	he/she/it		

Questions:

		Short Answers:	
Do I _____? Do we _____?	_____Yes, you do.	No, you don't.
Do you _____?	_____Yes, I do.	No, I don't.
	_____Yes, we do.	No, we don't.
Do they _____?	_____Yes, they do.	No, they don't.
Does he _____?	_____Yes, he does.	No, he doesn't.
Does she _____?	_____Yes, she does.	No, she doesn't.

Simple Present Wh Questions

A. These sentences are not true. Cross out the mistakes and say the sentences correctly.

Example: Jason plays baseball f~~our~~ days a week.
Jason plays baseball three days a week.

1. Jason and Todd play soccer on Monday.
2. Jason belongs to the Art Club.
3. Todd belongs to the Math Club.
4. Jason babysits for Amy on Tuesday.
5. Todd delivers mail.
6. Todd plays basketball on Tuesday.
7. Jason helps his mother at the drugstore.
8. Jason and Todd go to the laundromat on Thursday.
9. Jason visits his aunt on Thursday.
10. Only Todd delivers newspapers on Friday.

B. Answer these questions about Jason's and Todd's after-school activities.

on _____	every day

Example: When does Jason help his brother with the newspapers?
He helps his brother on Friday.

1. When does Jason help his mother with the food shopping?
2. When does Todd play basketball?
3. When do the boys have club meetings?
4. When does Todd deliver newspapers?
5. When does Todd go to his friend's house?
6. When does Jason have Science Club?
7. When do the boys go to the library?
8. When does Jason visit his grandmother?
9. When does Todd have Art Club?
10. When do the boys work together?

C. Answer these "Who" questions about the boys' after-school activities.

Jason does. Todd does.	Jason and Todd do.

1. Who plays baseball?
2. Who goes to the library?
3. Who helps his mother?
4. Who plays basketball on Wednesday?
5. Who delivers newspapers?
6. Who visits his grandmother?
7. Who goes to a club after school?
8. Who babysits for Tommy?
9. Who belongs to the Science Club?
10. Who has a busy week?

D. Ask and answer questions about Jason's and Todd's activities.

	does	Jason	do	
What		Todd	play	on _____?
Where			deliver	
	do	Jason and Todd	go	

Writing

A. Fill in each blank with the correct word.

does	do	play
does	go	deliver

1. When ___*do*___ Todd and Jason ___*play*___ baseball?

2. What _____ Todd _____ on Wednesday?

3. When _____ Todd _____ newspapers?

4. What _____ the boys _____ on Thursday?

5. When _____ the boys _____ to the library?

6. Where _____ the boys _____ on Thursday?

7. What _____ Jason _____ on Monday?

8. When _____ the boys _____ newspapers together?

9. Where _____ Jason _____ on Thursday?

10. When _____ Todd _____ to Art Club?

B. Put the words in these questions in order. Write the answer.

1. go / When / library / the / ? / do / the / boys / to

   ___When do the boys go to the library?___ ___On Thursday.___

2. plays / ? / basketball / Who

   _____ _____

3. Where / on / ? / boys / do / the / go / Thursday

   _____ _____

4. Jason / Friday / do / ? / does / on / What

   _____ _____

5. What / do / Monday / ? / do / boys / on / the

_____   _____

6. has / Art / Tuesday / Club / Who / on / ?

_____   _____

7. does / Friday / on / ? / Todd / go / Where

_____   _____

8. Jason / When / Science / ? / does / Club / have

_____   _____

9. What / ? / Todd / on / does / Tuesday / do

_____   _____

10. Todd / deliver / ? / does / When / newspapers

_____   _____

C. Circle the correct answer.

1. Who does Todd visit?   a. Todd does.   b. His grandmother.
2. Who visits his grandmother?   a. Todd does.   b. His grandmother.
3. Who helps his mother?   a. Jason does.   b. His mother.
4. Who does Jason help?   a. Jason does.   b. His mother.
5. Who babysits for Tommy?   a. Jason does.   b. Tommy.
6. Who does Jason babysit for?   a. Jason does.   b. Tommy.
7. Who does Todd play with?   a. Todd does.   b. Ben.
8. Who plays with Ben?   a. Todd does.   b. Ben.
9. Who does Jason help?   a. Jason does.   b. Todd.
10. Who helps Todd?   a. Jason does.   b. Todd.

D. Read the story. Then write the questions

JASON AND TODD

Jason and Todd are brothers. The boys are both in junior high school. Jason is 13. He's in 8th grade. Todd is 15. He's in 9th grade.

After school, the boys are always busy. Jason is a baseball player. He's on the school team. Jason plays first base, and he's fast and strong. He wants to be a baseball player in the major leagues.

Todd enjoys sports, too. He plays baseball and basketball after school, but he isn't on the school team. Every day at 4:30, Todd delivers newspapers. He delivers fifty newspapers in his area. On Friday afternoon, Jason helps him. Todd collects money from the customers, and Jason delivers the papers. With tips, Todd makes about $30 a week. Todd is saving for a computer. It costs about $1,500. He already has $900 in the bank.

1. What *does Jason do after school* ?   He plays baseball.

2. What _____ ?   A baseball player in the major leagues.

3. Who _____ ?   Todd does.

4. What _____ ?   He delivers newspapers.

5. How many newspapers _____ ?   Fifty.

6. When _____ ?   On Friday afternoon.

7. Who _____ ?   Jason does.

8. How much money _____ ?   About $30.

9. How much money _____ ? $900.

Grammar Summary

Simple Present Tense Wh Questions:

Questions:		Answers:	
When does Todd play basketball?	....	TIME	.... On Wednesday.
What does he do on Wednesday?	....	VERBS	.... Plays basketball.
What does he play on Wednesday?	....	OBJECT	.... Basketball.
Where do the boys go on Thursday?	....	PLACE	.... To the library.
Who(m) does Jason help on Wednesday?	....	PERSON	.... His mother.
Who helps his mother on Wednesday?	....	PERSON	.... Jason does.

When What	do	I/we/you/they	verb?
Where Who(m)	does	he/she/it	
		Who	verbs?

124

PAULA AND PATTY

Present Continuous vs. Simple Present

A. Patty is careful of her health, but Paula isn't. Read each sentence. Is it about Patty or Paula? Write the name you think is right.

Paula _____ 1. She smokes a pack of cigarettes a day.

_____ 2. She doesn't smoke.

_____ 3. She eats a lot of fruit and vegetables.

_____ 4. She loves junk food.

_____ 5. She drinks five cups of coffee a day.

_____ 6. She doesn't drink coffee.

_____ 7. She jogs two miles a day.

_____ 8. She doesn't jog.

_____ 9. She has a cold.

_____ 10. She doesn't eat junk food.

B. Answer these questions about the picture.

Yes, she is.	Yes, she does.
No, she isn't.	No, she doesn't.

1. Is Patty making a salad?
2. Is Patty jogging now?
3. Does she jog every day?
4. Is Patty drinking a cup of coffee now?
5. Does Patty eat a lot of junk food?
6. Does Paula eat a lot of junk food?
7. Does Paula jog with Patty?
8. Is Paula eating her dinner now?
9. Is she eating a salad?
10. Is she eating a hamburger and french fries?

C. Read each sentence. Circle "R" if the action is <u>routine</u>. Circle "N" if the action is happening <u>now</u>.

	Routine	Now
1. Paula is drinking a cup of coffee.	R	(N)
2. Paula drinks five cups of coffee a day.	R	N
3. Patty and Paula are talking in the kitchen.	R	N
4. They talk in the kitchen every day.	R	N
5. Patty is wearing sneakers.	R	N
6. She wears shoes at work.	R	N
7. Paula is eating a hamburger and fries.	R	N
8. Patty eats a lot of fruit and vegetables.	R	N
9. Paula smokes a pack of cigarettes a day.	R	N
10. Paula is smoking a cigarette.	R	N

D. Use this chart. Ask and answer questions about the picture. Then, give a short answer.

Is	Patty	smoking? jogging? drinking coffee?
Does	Paula	smoke? jog? drink coffee?

Example: Is Patty drinking coffee?
No, she isn't.

Writing

A. Circle the correct form of the verb.

1. Patty (is making) makes a salad now.
2. She **is making** makes a salad every night.
3. Paula **is smoking** smokes now.
4. Paula **is smoking** smokes a pack of cigarettes a day.
5. Paula **is eating** eats a hamburger now.
6. She **is eating** eats junk food every night.
7. Paula **is taking** takes some cough medicine now.
8. She **is taking** takes cough medicine three times a day.
9. Patty **is wearing** wears jogging clothes now.
10. She **is wearing** wears jogging clothes after work.

B. Write the verb in the correct tense.

talk   1. Patty and Paula _____*are talking*_____ in the kitchen now.

2. They _____ every evening after work.

wear   3. Patty _____ her sneakers now.

4. She _____ shoes at work.

smoke   5. Paula _____ a cigarette now.

6. She _____ a pack of cigarettes a day.

drink   7. Paula _____ five cups of coffee a day.

8. She _____ a cup of coffee now.

make   9. Patty _____ a salad now.

10. Patty _____ a salad every night for dinner.

C. Read the story. Then, answer the questions.

PAULA AND PATTY

Patty and Paula are sisters, but they don't feel the same about their health and their diet. Patty worries about Paula. Paula gets sick a lot.

Patty pays attention to her diet. She eats fruit and vegetables, chicken and fish. She doesn't use salt or sugar in her food. Patty also exercises. She jogs every day after work. She swims at the local pool in the summertime.

Paula doesn't pay attention to her diet. She has two cups of coffee and a donut for breakfast. Sometimes she eats lunch; sometimes she doesn't. She stops at a fast food restaurant every night after work and picks up a hamburger, chicken or pizza for dinner.

Patty and Paula are in the kitchen, and they're talking. Patty is saying, "Come on, Paula. You're getting sick. You cough all the time, and you're getting fat. Stop smoking and stop the junk food. Come out and jog with me." Paula is saying, "I don't know. I'm very tired after work. I don't have much energy."

1. Are Patty and Paula sisters? _Yes, they are._

2. Do they agree about health and diet? _____

3. Are they talking in the kitchen now? _____

4. Does Patty jog every day? _____

5. Does Paula jog with Patty? _____

6. Does Paula eat lunch every day? _____

7. Are Patty and Paula talking now? _____

8. Is Paula getting heavy? _____

9. Does Patty care about Paula's health? _____

10. Does Paula feel tired after work? _____

D. Answer these questions about yourself.

1. Do you smoke? _____

2. Are you smoking now? _____

3. Do you jog? _____

4. Do you drink coffee? _____

5. Are you drinking a cup of coffee now? _____

6. Do you eat a lot of fruit and vegetables? _____

7. Do you like junk food? _____

8. Are you having a snack now? _____

9. Do you work? _____

10. Do you get tired after work? _____

11. Are you getting tired now? _____

Grammar Summary

The Present Continuous vs. The Simple Present:

In the present continuous tense, the action of the verb is happening "now".
In the simple present tense, the action happens "every day" (routinely).
Paula is smoking in the picture. Also, she smokes every day.
Patty isn't smoking, because she doesn't smoke.
Patty jogs every day, but she isn't jogging in this picture.

I	am am not	verbing.
He/She/It	is isn't	
We/You/They	are aren't	
I/We/You/They		verb.
	don't	verb
He/She/It		verbs.
	doesn't	verb.

SPORTS

Can (Ability)

1. _____

2. _____

3. _____

4. _____

5. _____

6. _____

7. _____

8. _____

A. Write the action under the correct picture of each sport.

swim	play tennis
ski	play soccer
lift weights	play baseball
ice skate	ride a bicycle

B. Use this chart. Make true sentences about the pictures.

Examples: Ali can play soccer.
Patty and Teresa can't ice skate.

Michael		lift weights.
Ali	can	play tennis.
Patty		play soccer.
Teresa	can't	ice skate.
Michael and Ali		ride a bicycle.
Patty and Teresa		play baseball.

C. Answer these questions about the pictures.

Yes, s/he can.	Yes, they can.	Yes, I can.
No, s/he can't.	No, they can't.	No, I can't.

1. Can Michael swim?
2. Can Ali swim?
3. Can Michael play soccer?
4. Can Michael and Ali ride bicycles?
5. Can they lift weights?

6. Can Patty ski?
7. Can Teresa ice skate?
8. Can Patty and Teresa play tennis?
9. Can you swim?
10. Can you ski?

D. Make sentences with "but" about these pictures.

Examples: Michael can swim, but Ali can't.
Michael can't play soccer, but Ali can.

3. Michael   Teresa

4. Ali   Patty

5. Patty   Ali

6. Teresa   Michael

Writing

A. Paul is an athlete. He loves sports. George isn't an athlete. He hates sports. Write about Paul and George.

Paul   George

1. Paul _can swim_ well.   George _can't swim_ at all.
   (swim)

2. Paul _____ well.   George _____ at all.
   (play tennis)

3. Paul _____ well.   George _____ at all.
   (lift weights)

4. Paul _____ well.   George _____ at all.
   (surf)

5. Paul _____ well.   George _____ at all.
   (play baseball)

6. Paul _____ well.   George _____ at all.
   (ice skate)

7. Paul _____ well.   George _____ at all.
   (play soccer)

8. Paul _____ well.   George _____ at all.
   (ski)

B. Write a question for each picture.

Example:

Can Michael ski?

No, he can't.

2. _____

Yes, he can.

4. _____

Yes, they can.

6. _____

Yes, he can.

8. _____

No, she can't.

Patty

_____

Yes, she can.

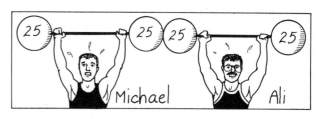

25   25 25   25

Michael   Ali

3. _____

No, they can't.

Teresa

5. _____

No, she can't.

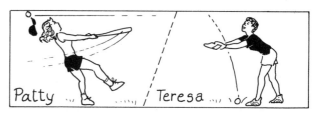

Patty   Teresa

7. _____

No, they can't.

Ali

9. _____

No, he can't

C. Write a sentence with "but" about each picture.

Example:

Michael can swim, but Patty can't.

1. _____

2. _____

3. _____

4. _____

5. _____

6. _____

7. _____

8. _____

9. _____

10. _____

D. Answer these questions about yourself.

| Yes, I can. | No, I can't. |

1. Can you swim? _____

2. Can you play soccer? _____

3. Can you ride a bicycle? _____

4. Can you lift weights? _____

5. Can you ski? _____

6. Can you ice skate? _____

7. Can you play tennis? _____

8. Can you play baseball? _____

Grammar Summary

The Modal Auxilliary Verb CAN

1. The negative of "can" is "cannot" or "can't".

2. In this unit "can" = permanent ability, skill, or know-how.
   "I can speak English." = "I have the ability. I know how."
   "I can't speak Chinese." = "I don't have the ability. I don't know how."

3. In this unit, "can" and "can't" show present time.

Affirmative and Negative Statements:

Michael can swim.
Ali can't swim.
Patty and Teresa can play tennis.

I He She It We You They	can can't cannot	verb	(_____).

Michael can swim, but Ali can't.
Patty and Teresa can play tennis, but Michael and Ali can't.

I He She It We You They	can can't	verb	(_____),	but	I he she it we you they	can't. can.

APPENDIX

Cardinal Numbers

0 zero		
1 one	11 eleven	21 twenty-one
2 two	12 twelve	22 twenty-two
3 three	13 thirteen	23 twenty-three
4 four	14 fourteen	24 twenty-four
5 five	15 fifteen	25 twenty-five
6 six	16 sixteen	26 twenty-six
7 seven	17 seventeen	27 twenty-seven
8 eight	18 eighteen	28 twenty-eight
9 nine	19 nineteen	29 twenty-nine
10 ten	20 twenty	30 thirty

40 forty	60 sixty	80 eighty
50 fifty	70 seventy	90 ninety
		100 one hundred

Ordinal Numbers

1st first	eleventh	twentieth
2nd second	twelfth	thirtieth
3rd third	thirteenth	fortieth
4th fourth	fourteenth	fiftieth
5th fifth	fifteenth	sixtieth
6th sixth		
7th seventh	sixteenth	seventieth
8th eighth	seventeenth	eightieth
9th ninth	eighteenth	ninetieth
10th tenth	nineteenth	one hundredth

Spelling Rules
Present Continuous

1. Regular Spelling
   walk — walking
   eat — eating
   cook — cooking
   carry — carrying

2. Consonant + Final "e"
   drive — driving
   write — writing
   smoke — smoking

3. Consonant + vowel + consonant
   (one-syllable words)
   put — putting
   sit — sitting
   stop — stopping

4. Verbs ending with "w", "x" and "y"
   fix — fixing
   buy — buying

5. Verbs ending in "ie"
   lie — lying
   tie — tying